Striving for Equality Freedom and Justice

Embracing Roots, Culture and Identity

A Collection of Poetry

Zita Holbourne

Poet~Artist~Activist

HANSIB

First published in Great Britain by Hansib Publications in 2016

Hansib Publications Limited
P.O. Box 226, Hertford
Hertfordshire SG14 3WY UK

info@hansibpublications.com
www.hansibpublications.com

ISBN 978-1-910553-56-5

A CIP catalogue record for this book
is available from the British Library

Production by Hansib Publications Limited
Printed in Great Britain

DEDICATION

This book is dedicated to my pride, hero, inspiration and the person who keeps my spirit strong and determined every day, my son T.C.C.

CONTENTS

PREFACE

Roots, Culture, Identity is a collection of poems, quotes and illustrations created by the author, as part of her quest for equality freedom and justice. Zita is frequently described as a political poet and a griot of the struggle. Zita's roles as a poet, artist and activist are intertwined and interconnected and the book reflects her life as a campaigner. This book is a must read for all lovers of poetry and spoken word. But it is also for all those who have lived through struggle, all those who have survived through challenges and grown stronger and for those who seek encouragement and inspiration to keep on keeping on. 'The poems in the book together with Zita's artworks and quotes, weave a story of history to the present day to hopes for the future.' The poems in the book switch between personal stories to a historical and a modern day documentation of the struggle against discrimination, injustice, austerity and poverty told in verse.

ACKNOWLEDGMENTS

I would like to acknowledge all those who went before, those who sacrificed lives and life times, who remain an inspiration long after they have passed. I would like to thank my family, especially my son who is the 'shine in my sun', and all those who stand in solidarity and unity against oppression, discrimination and injustice every day, those who have encouraged me so that I was able to arm myself with the courage to step forward and rise up with confidence and last but most definitely not least my sistas and brothas who stand should to shoulder with me - my spiritual family. I also give thanks to Arif Ali and Hansib Publications for publishing my work and for being part of my journey.

ABOUT THE AUTHOR

Zita Holbourne is an award winning UK based spoken word artist / poet, visual artist, curator, writer and trade union, community and human rights activist/campaigner.

She is known as a Political Poet and a Griot of the Struggle, was part of a Brixton based black poetry collective in the 1990s and resident poet and co-host of Nu Whirled Voyces. Her poetry has been featured on TV and Radio and she has performed at a broad range of events including awards ceremonies, several Blue Plaque unveilings commemorating the lives of black historical figures, the official UK memorial service for Nelson Mandela and the Glastonbury festival. She has won a range of awards for her poetry and was a finalist / one of 5 People's Choice Poets in the Manorlogz Xtreme Spoken Word Contest.

Zita studied graphic design at the London College of Printing and has worked as a freelance graphic designer and make-up artist. She exhibits at a broad range of political, cultural and community events and curates art exhibitions to challenge discrimination and injustice and showcase young black, and migrant artists.

Zita is elected to the Public and Commercial Services (PCS) Union National Executive Committee, the TUC Race Relations Committee, The Action for Southern Africa (successor to the Anti-Apartheid Movement) National Executive Council and the Movement Against Xenophobia National Steering Group. She is the Co-Founder and National Co-Chair of Black Activists Rising Against Cuts (BARAC) UK, a national organisation which campaigns against the disproportionate impact of cuts and austerity on black workers, service users and communities and against the discrimination and injustice faced by black communities. *Black is used in the political sense to include all people from the African and Asian diasporas.* Zita is a founding member of several anti-racist, equality and anti-austerity movements and organisations in the UK.

In 2012 Zita won the Positive Role Model for Race Award at the National Diversity Awards. In 2013 Zita was listed as one of the

Afro News top 12 African and Caribbean women of the year and has been nominated in the Eight Women Awards. Zita is one of 14 women campaigners featured in the book Here We Stand, Women Changing the World, published by Honno Press which won the Bread and Roses Award for Radical Publishing in 2015.

Websites: www.zitaholbourne.blogspot.com
www.blackactivistsrisingagainstcuts.blogspot.com
YouTube: 'ZitaPoetActivist'
SoundCloud: https://soundcloud.com/zita-holbourne

'Mother Africa'
Ink on canvas

CHAPTER 1

THE ROOTS OF HER-STORY, HIS-STORY, *OUR* STORY

Roots, cultures, identities, separate entities
But underpinning and intertwining all three, is a strong
sense of what makes me – me.

REDEFINING HISTORY

We, our parents, our grandparents, came to this country
And in half a century redefined Britain's history
Arriving by ship enthusiastically
We were greeted by the mist and the grey of the sea

The bitter cold of the winter season
Was nothing compared to the ice cold freezing
Attitude of those in this country
Full of hatred and hostility

Greeted by signs of 'Keep Britain White'
We'd come unprepared for a fight
'No dogs, no Irish, no blacks'
We had to always watch our backs

We were told this was the mother country
What mother uses terms that are derogatory?
What kind of mother rejects
And sets out to inject

A sense of worthlessness
Within the child she should caress?
For fifty years we've struggled and fought
Sometimes defiant, sometimes distraught

To make a place and be accepted
As young or old and black and gifted
And look what we've achieved
Despite having to live aggrieved

We built and developed the NHS
Made London Transport one of the best
Established a carnival while we were oppressed
That's now renowned as Europe's largest

'Caribbean Sunset'
acrylic on canvas

Facing fascism and humiliation
Tackling racism and discrimination
Just look what we've achieved
Despite having to live aggrieved

We've excelled within this land
That refused a helping hand
In spreading the word of the Holy Scriptures
In trade unions and in literature

In sports and politics
In broadcasting and music
In entertainment and education
We helped empower this nation

Despite the fact we were deceived
We came and we achieved

We, our parents, our grandparents
Came to this country
And in half a century
Redefined Britain's history
Re-defined-Bri-tain's -his-to-ry! ✤

EXILED IN EAST LONDON

From West African shores to the Caribbean
Exile of an enslaved human being
From Caribbean shores
To England's closed doors
Bearing signs of 'No dogs, no Irish, no blacks'
Shouting out 'go back
To where you came from'
Assuming my home's a land of sugar and rum

Where I'm from is a mixture of
African roots, Caribbean trunk, Spanish, French and British
     branches
A family tree of oppression, circumstance and chances

I can't go back without tracing my ancestral footprints
Without carrying out DNA tests to determine my fore parents
What I know is my spirit is African
My heart is Caribbean
But best of all I'm a human being

Born here, but never accepted
Because no one ever expected
Me to claim Britain as my own
Even though it's my 'born and bred' home
'Where you from love?' man in the shop asked
I decided to have some fun and laughed
'East London' straight faced I tell him
'Well I knew you was born 'ere but like foreign'
He says matter of fact
I cast aside tact
Ask him 'How can I be foreign if I'm born here?'
But as I turn away angrily in my eye there's a tear

Exiled in East London
Exiled in my birth Kingdom
Enslavement of my ancestors still determining for some my worth
Forever I'll be deemed an exile in the land of my birth ❧

NO APOLOGY

Chained and enslaved
Sold and contained
No Apology!

Lynchings and Jim Crow laws
Glass ceilings and closed doors
No Apology!

Colonial rule and centuries of oppression
Racist attack upon attack in succession
No Apology!

Apartheid and segregation
Inequality and discrimination
No Apology!

Poor housing, low pay
Racist abuse day after day
No Apology!

Ignorance and prejudice
Bigotry and injustice
No Apology!

Brutal killings with no remorse
Treated as inferior and viewed as worse
No Apology!

National Front and the BNP
Far right politicians on TV
No Apology!

Top Gear and David Starkey
Offensive names like wog, paki and darky
No Apology!

Stop and search, racial profiling
Workplace harassment and bullying
No Apology!

Attacking multiculturalism
Institutional racism
No Apology!

But when a black politician posts a tweet online
She's wrongly accused of committing a racist crime
Whilst all we've experienced is expected to be forgiven
This is the response I believe she should have given;
NO A – PO-LO-GY! ❧

SURVIVOR GUILT

Want to sleep but so many emotions filling my mind
Thinking about those ripped apart from me then left behind
It pains not knowing if they lived or died
If those who gave assurances lied
If they're suffering still, forced to be slaves
Or lying in makeshift unmarked graves

Ridden with guilt that I was allowed to survive
Not understanding how it is that I'm still alive
I left with nothing apart from the memories in my head
I recall the stench on the roadside of those lying dead
I still feel the familiarity of the heat and the dust
The uncertainty of not knowing who to trust

Torn between the fear of being alone
And returning to what was once my home
Here in this land of grey clouds, hostility and strangers
It's hard to distinguish between safe spaces and dangers
I long for the security of my mother's embrace
Her quiet resilience and natural grace

The laughter in her voice and warmth of her smile
If I close my eyes she's with me for a while
This is why I don't like to sleep as in my dreams all's well
Until each time I must awake to face this living hell
Of isolation, homesickness, loss and survivor guilt
And the unfamiliar feel of a warm winter quilt ❧

TEARS FOR PALESTINE

Crying for the lives that were stolen
Crying for the hearts that were broken
Denied an opportunity to blossom
Crying for the mother holding her lifeless child to her bosom
Crying for the father who tried to protect his family
Crying for these crimes against humanity

But my sorrow can't bring back loved ones torn from this earth
My tears cannot cultivate a rebirth
So as I dry my eyes
I pledge to organise
For an end to the occupation
And the right to self determination

Recall my own childhood fights
For my own human rights
Stripped of my home but never my dignity
Stripped of my rights but never my identity
Resilience an inbuilt ability
I can be displaced but I'm still part of a community

Roots, cultures, identities
Separate entities
But intertwining and underpinning all three
Is a strong sense of what make me me

No weapon or occupation
Can wipe out the existence of a nation
Where they began is embedded in time
History cannot be erased by inhumane crime
But the scales of justice will only balance
When we rise as one, organise and challenge

Until the attacks on them cease
Until the people of Palestine can live at ease
My tears will be replaced with solidarity
Until peace for Palestine becomes a reality ❧

TRIBUTE TO THE ANTI-APARTHEID MOVEMENT

It's fifty years since they began
It started with campaigns to ban
South African goods during apartheid
And drew in strength as it opened our eyes
To the wicked and cruel white supremacy regime
As we realised things aren't always what they seem

Like enslavement and segregation
Good strong people all took action
Boycotting goods and demonstrating
Raising awareness and campaigning
Seeking justice and equality
Release, peace and democracy

For the freedom fighters, black, Asian and white
Who strived for a fair South Africa in sight
Some exiled, some incarcerated
Striving to be emancipated
Second class citizens in their own lands
Oppressed by the colour bans

'No Barclays Bank and No Cape Fruit!'
Campaigning to give Botha the boot
'Freeeeee- eee Nelson Man-De-Laaaa!'
Marching, chanting **'Amaaand-La!'**

On the curb in Trafalgar Square
Anti-apartheid movement dare
To demonstrate outside South Africa House
Its leaders with their powerful words rouse

'No Robin Island! No colour divide!'
'No trading whilst there's apartheid!'

Young and old, black and white
Students, workers, all unite

To end the evil apartheid regime
The AAM created a powerful team

Raising awareness around the world
Calling the leaders to join, be heard
Make a stand and stop trading
Bring an end to the hating

2009 and its fifty years
Since AAM opened our eyes and ears
To understand and realise
Our responsibility to rise!
And to take action and secure freedom
For those imprisoned in their own kingdom

Hope for black people oppressed across earth
'Get Up! Stand up! For their rights stripped from birth
The Anti-Apartheid Movement was a lesson to us all
Showing how together we could force a tyrannical rule to fall
Raise awareness and bring about equality
'Free at last! Free at last! Set Our People Free!

With time, healing and determination
Father Mandela, the backing of a nation
The day came – South Africa was emancipated
From its terrible rule of fascism and hatred
The Anti-Apartheid Movement and its supporters
Celebrated with South Africa's sons and daughters
Commended for their efforts by the Madiba
For now was an end to a terrible era

But with apartheid gone
The struggles still went on
And Action for Southern Africa was formed
To support the region as it was reformed

Amandla Awethu! AAM and ACTSA
Thanks for supporting beautiful South Africa ✄

HAITI; FREEDOM AND SURVIVAL

Descendent from black Jacobins
Who were descendent from enslaved Africans
Who led the Haitian Revolution
Whilst there were five degrees of segregation
Big Whites, Small Whites, Mullatoes, Free Blacks and Slaves
Captained by the fearless and brave
Toussaint L'Overture
Not willing to endure
Enslavement's oppression
Rejected outright being someone's possession
Some say thirteen is an unlucky number
But this is the number of years it took to conquer
First Caribbean Republic ruled by people of African ancestry
Eliminated French colonial rule and set themselves free

Tumultuous history
Drowning in poverty
Political unrest
Putting a Nation to the test
Now plagued by nature's wrath
Struggling for survival in the aftermath

Lives lost once again on the scale of the revolution
For those who have passed there's no solution
Two hundred years ago bloodshed, lives sacrificed in the name of
    freedom
Two hundred years later lives lost for no good reason

What the ancestors fought to keep, nature has taken away
Leaving the survivors in turmoil and disarray
The revolution could not be televised but the earthquake aftermath
    is now
Whilst various agencies and authorities debate the when, where
    and how
Many have died, others are dying
Homeless, wounded, crying

Their impoverished state couldn't have prepared them for nature's
   tremoring heart
Now the battle's not for freedom but survival, as living has become
   an art ❧

THE FAR AWAY BEAT OF AN ANCESTRAL DRUM

This is a tribute
To those who did contribute
To popular music's birth
In the twentieth century
In celebration of our people's history

We never left our roots behind
And what has really struck my mind
Is how it began with a drum beat
Our communication link when we could not meet

When enslavement tore us from the mother land
This African beat joined with rhythm hand in hand
Creating a new musical sensation
Our people gave birth to their new creation

Developing a new sound explosion
Heartfelt and loaded with deep emotion
Jazz was the name of this new sound sensation
It encompassed all the suffering of our now scattered nation

Jazz was the celebration of a new generation
Rising up from slavery
Expressing their creativity

From Louis Armstrong's trumpet blowing
To John Coltrane's sax solos flowing
From Jelly Roll Morton's rag time sensation
To Charlie Parker's improvisation
From Duke Ellington's big band sound
To Billie Holiday's emotions abound
From Mile's Davis's cool originality
To Ella Fitzgerald's smooth vocal delivery

These jazz performers all became
Legendary gaining worldwide respect and reclaim

So people of all races knew their name
And celebrated the sound that rose from
The faraway beat of an ancestral drum

And through the generations this sound grew up to be
The mother of popular music now our people were all free
So in celebration of our people's history
I pay tribute to what we've achieved musically ✖

SAME VISION

Does it matter that you worship a God by a different name from me
For in many ways we are the same, wouldn't you agree?
The different tongues we speak in only determine where we have been
Throughout the history of time for isn't your past the same as mine?
Are we not the sons and daughters
Of the mothers and fathers
Who were there at the start
Before enslavement tore us apart?
Travelling along separate roads
Establishing different abodes
Not through our own decision
But because of enforced oppression

Our reasons for being here are diverse
And sometimes it seems like a horrific curse
Having to live and progress in a place
Where we are prejudged because of our race
Looked upon and treated as though we are inferior
By the racists in this land who think they are superior

The struggle goes on still, trying to survive
We're fighting for the right to have peace within our lives
So why when we're faced with discrimination
And hatred from this nation
Do we allow such a division?
Between our own people, when we share the same vision
Of eliminating the racism, that for so long we've had to face
Why, oh why are we fighting and killing people of our own race

We have to support one another
Unite and remain together
If we are going to beat
The prejudice and defeat
The evil racists trying to prevent
Our people from rising from this bitter lament

We've got to stick together and unite
Bring our vision into sight
Keep the bond between us tight
If we want to overcome the plight

There are differences between us and that fact we must accept
Btu it shouldn't create conflict, instead we should respect
Our individual thoughts and beliefs
And stop causing each other so much grief

We've got to unite
Keep our vision in sight
Work together for what's right
Our right to live in peace
And for the racism to cease

Just remember where we came from
We began strong and proud as one
The racist slave owners created our division
Let's turn it around and achieve our vision ❧

'Every Day is Mother's Day'
Acrylic on canvas board

CHAPTER 2

MY IDENTITY; AIN'T I A WOMAN?

I don't have the option of separating my gender from my race or my race from my gender, both are an important part of who I am but I cannot be defined by gender or race alone as I am so much more.

WHO AM I

I am an African
I am a Nubian
Regal like a queen
From before time began I descend
From time's nether regions I ascend
Like a vision I transcend

I am a mother, a daughter
I exist to nurture
I am an adventurer
I am a conqueror

Yet I am full of compassion
I thrive on passion
Always in vogue
Never out of fashion

I am Mother Nature's kin
For ever conscious of where I have been
Throughout the history of time
I have remained divine
Often oppressed
Sometimes obsessed
Awesome a magical sorceress
Able to recreate in my own image
I never began and I will never finish
In my surety I trust my premonition
To take me forward to my beginning
Never losing, never winning
Never conceited, never defeated
I breed success, repent, confess
Recreate, procreate and elate in my eternal state

Historic stones are engraved with my blood
Rivers form into oceans from my monthly flood
I am mother to the generations
All that are living and have lived are my creation

I am older than time
Forever in my prime
A sage with no age
Although wizened
I still indulge myself in knowledge
And divulge my past and my beginnings
With each new innings
I lament but am forgiving
Never losing, never winning
Never conceited
Never defeated
I place no limitation on my embrace
Not religion or culture or race

I am a creator
A part of nature
My womb defines my role
Supremacy my ultimate goal

I am a woman and I am free
To redefine my role throughout the history
I am timeless and ageless
I create my own status
Love is my desire
Knowledge my private empire

Forming and formulating
Stating and situating
Connecting and perfecting my existence
With persistence
When all that have thrived in my womb
Enter a sudden and bitter doom
Place in a battle for survival
I breathe only for their revival

I cannot go back nor can I end
Therefore I must naturally transcend
With each second, each hour, each year
As each new century draws near
And digest all that I have seen
Contemplate who and what I have been

A *vision, a miracle, a wonder*
I am rain, sun, wind and thunder
I am the oceans, I am the mountains
I am a seedling, a forest, a tropical storm
A desert, a glacier
Each new born creature
Each landscape's feature
A moment, *a breath*
Each sudden death
A volcano, an earthquake
A rainbow, moonlight
Each scent, each sound, each taste, each sight

Who am I?
The creator of birth
Simply
I am
Sweet
Mother **Earth** ❧

WOMAN

WOMAN has to hold a family together
WOMAN still stays calm at the end of her tether
WOMAN has to balance being mother with a job
Come home cook and clean, she's so tired she could drop

Then she goes back out to work to do an evening shift
She can't even stop for coffee to give herself a lift
She comes home late at night, hoping that she'll get some rest
But her man wants attention, *so she massages his chest.*

When she finally gets to sleep, morning time is almost here
Then the baby wakes up crying and it's more than she can bear.
His daddy's sleeping deeply, so it's mother who must rise
As she feeds her hungry child she wipes the sleep from her eyes

WOMAN has to suffer once a month with hormone change
But no one makes allowance for her awful aching pains.
WOMAN HAS TO CARRY FOR NINE MONTHS HER
    GROWING CHILD
She still works though she's tired and the pain has turned her wild
She just carries on as usual with a smile upon her face
And though she feels her back is breaking, she still holds herself
    with grace

With her kinfolk still demanding that she does the household chores
She still goes out to work, then gets the groceries from the stores
With her unborn kicking hard she hurries through the pouring rain
Grasping hard the heavy bags she wonders if she'll turn insane
When at last she's home, the work is still not done
For her family's demanding has only just begun
She changes from a chef to a waitress to a maid
As she looks into the future she can't help but feel afraid
All she wants is some enjoyment or at least some gratitude
But it's gonna take a lot for man to change his attitude

Now the time has come for her infant to be born
She screams aloud with pain as she feels herself being torn
After agonising hours of contractions and no sleep
She doesn't know if she should laugh or if she should weep
As she holds her baby tight
She smiles on her with delight

WOMAN IS A PLEASURE, A WONDER OF THE EARTH
Without her there would be no us, for **WOMAN** does give birth
WOMAN is a treasure, a beauty to behold
She's strong and brave and loving, worth much much more than
    GOLD ✣

MY BLACK IS BEAUTY FULL

She shouted; **My black is beautiful!**
MY. BLACK. IS. BEAUTY. FULL!
Attacks on it are institutional
Designed to make her feel inferior
But as well as beautiful she has a tough exterior

Her black has been denigrated
She's been discriminated
Against because of the colour of her skin
Sometimes even by her own kin

Treated as though the smooth sheen
Makes her an inferior human being
At home they called her the ugly one
Never considering the damage done

To her confidence and self esteem
At school they didn't seem
To recognise her beauty
Never a princess always a tree

In the school productions she longed to play
A part that put her beauty on display
But indoctrinated with the belief
That she was worthless she embraced her grief

Silently assuming she had no right
And kept her beauty out of sight
Covering up with clothing
Secretly loathing
Her appearance and being
She stopped believing
In herself and her ability
Regarded her skin colour as a disability

When doors closed and opportunity didn't knock
She decided to lock
Herself away, cut off from others
No friends, no lovers

Her family worried and now feeling guilty
Far too late realised they'd acted disgracefully
Ashamed they purchased tickets for a flight
Reluctantly she travelled in the night

Where at least she could remain hidden
Under the night flight light's dim
She awoke apprehensive of what this new place might bring
As she peered down below over the plane's wing

She saw golden sands that glistened against
The turquoise sea on the descent
So inviting she longed to be there
Then sadly remembered she would have to bear

Her ugliness to do so
And knew she'd never go
What happened when she arrived
She could never have believed

In the airport at first she didn't realise
That the beautiful people before her eyes
Had the same dark skin she had
She was just glad

To be surrounded by such uplifting
People smiling and insisting
That she have a wonderful stay
Complementing her on her way

One woman told her mother
She was blessed to have a daughter
With so beautiful a complexion
At first she didn't make the connection

That the daughter
Was in fact her
Young men eyed her with admiration
Older men looked on with resignation

Wishing they were 20 or 30 years younger
Young women looked enviously at her
And slowly she began to recognise
The attention bestowed on her and realise
That she must in fact not be so ugly after all
Especially when the young men lined up to call
At her grandmother's house where they came to stay
And every day she heard Gran say

The words she first said when they got there
'I used to have the beauty you have my dear'
'Now I am old and you are young'
'Your black is beautiful dear one'

And now she could believe it was true
Each day here she grew
Amongst her people blessed by the sun's glow
A new high replaced her lifetime low

This place fitted her like a glove
And it was here she found her first love
And as they sat on golden sands and watched the sun set
She became overwhelmed and leapt

To her feet with joy in a daze
She danced in and out of the waves
In her new bikini flung her arms up in the air
She felt no sorrow or fear

And shouted loudly 'My black is beautiful'
'MY. BLACK. IS. BEAUTY. FULL!' ✄

OUT OF THE SHADOWS

Out of the shadows she is light
Out of the shadows shining bright
Out of the shadows she steps gingerly
Out of the shadows desperately
Hoping that she can be free
To be the best she can be

She has been hidden for so long
Although she did nothing wrong
She was persecuted and demonised
By those who hated, abused and lied
Drove her to sorrow and despair
Living in pain and fear

Out of the shadows cautiously
Yet still she holds herself regally
She carries herself elegantly
Dresses herself beautifully
And takes that first step through
Knowing that this is the right thing to do

She wraps her head with grace
Adorns herself with fine lace
Oils her skin of chocolate milk
Layers her body in satin and silk
Multi-coloured fabrics divine
And prays that she will shine ❧

MONTHLY INSANITY

I'm feeling all worried and hot
And I'm sweating a bit, *no a lot!*
My hair is a mess and I feel under stress
And I can't go out wearing this dress

I just want to wallow alone in self-pity
And I hate living here in this terrible city
Nobody loves me and nobody cares
And I can't stop myself from shedding these tears

I want to go out; *no I want to stay in*
I want to eat cake *but I want to get thin*
I hate being me; I don't know what to do
I thought you loved me, but know now we're through

I don't want to work and I don't want to live
I'm stupid and worthless and I've nothing to give
Get me some chocolate – now! Straight away!
If you don't then I warn you, you're gonna pay

Now get out of my sight and turn off the light
No I don't want to go out clubbing tonight
My stomach is bloated, I'm covered in zits
I've eaten too much and it's all on my hips

I just want to lie down and get rid of this pain
These cramps are so awful, I'm going insane
What do you mean; *it's only the time of the month*
Get out of my sight or I'll give you a thump! ❧

MY BODY, MY GENDER, MY RIGHT

I wept for all the abuses of my sisters and me
Thought about how this horrible situation could be
Taking advantage of our youth and insecurity
Preying on our innocence and vulnerability

Girls, women of all ages, religions, races
This shouldn't be the reality each one faces
Our daughters should not be the ones taught to be aware
Our sons should be raised to be respectful and care

About the lives of the daughters, mothers
Nieces and grandmothers of others
As they should for their own female relations
And work to prevent these situations

That girls and women have faced for eternity
Treat every single one with respect and dignity
Are they not the sons of mothers, the fathers of daughters?
So why treat other women like lambs to the slaughter

My body is my temple not for another to use
I did not come to be on this earth for another to abuse
The deepened scars my sisters bare are with them for life
Stretching across their souls like a raw wound from a knife

What happened can never be reversed or undone
Not something they can hide or run away from
Some memories never fade haunting in quiet times
Whilst those responsible go unpunished for their crimes

Knowing they are human rights abusers
Yet wearing their crimes like badges of honour
Or when exposed acting like the victim is them
From where does their twisted thinking and mentality stem?

If we don't work collectively to tackle the root causes
We condemn our girl children to a cycle of abuses
Mothers and fathers start by teaching your boy children
To be respectful and make sure they learn and listen

My gender, my body and my right
To dignity, freedom, day & night
My sisters should be free to dress as they please
To experience life freely and with ease

Embrace their femininity with joy and pride
Express who they are proudly, not run or hide
No man has the right to demand or dictate
Women were not placed on this earth for men to take. ✤

'Jazz'
Acrylic & Ink on canvas

CHAPTER 3

CULTURALLY AWARE

I refuse to be boxed, labelled or categorised. I am more than your eye can see. My uniqueness is not a weakness. Originality is not abnormality.

UNDEFINABLE

When you look at me, what do you see?
An individual filled with pride and dignity
When you look at me what do you see?
An individual facing up to my responsibility?
When you look at me what are you seeing?
Do you see a person, simply a human being?

Or do you see me as a mother or somebody's wife?
What assumptions are you making on how I live my life?
Do you see me as a half caste, mulatto or mixed race?
Or simply as a human being who holds herself with grace?

Do you wonder at my age
Why I'm not married or at least engaged?
Do you cast a critical eye
And do you wonder why
I have a child but no wedding band?
Do you think you can judge me by looking at my hand?

Did the father leave me or did I leave him?
Do you think that perhaps I am 'living in sin'?
Am I a single mother, a one parent family?
Just what do you see?

Do you observe what I wear?
Is it an issue or do you not care?
Whether I wear a designer dress
Or simply believe in dressing for less?

Do you wonder if I have a good job?
Or if I go out and rob
Judging me simply by what I own
Do you expect me to have a nice home?
Or expect me to sign on every two weeks
Just because of the way I look and speak?

Does my career make me middle class?
Or am I working class because of my rearing and past?
Or am I simply classless because I am unique
Or does being like no one else make me some kind of freak?

Do you see me as a statistic?
Is you assessment of me realistic?
Why do you prejudge me from the way I look?
Don't judge me by my cover, open up the book

You cannot necessarily judge me by what your eye can see
Does it matter if I'm living in wealth or in poverty?
Does it matter if I own my own home or rent from the local authority?
Does it make a difference if I'm married or not
So long as I'm responsible for and love my kids a lot

Do you have the right to ascertain my colour, culture or creed?
Is it not for me to decide and for you to follow my lead?
Regardless of class, regardless of status
We all start of the same when our parents create us

Don't look at me and decide
Who you think I am inside
It takes more to define what I comprise of
Than simply by opening your eyes up

I am undefinable, yet I am still desirable
You cannot categorise me and say
Because of a label I should act a certain way

I am classy and classless
I create my own status
For ever changing like a season
My life is not for you to reason. ✺

MULTICULTURALISM

I embrace my multiculturalism
As I do my Afrocentrism
As I do my Feminism
And even my Englishism

I have African and European roots but I'm a Londoner
I'm both Caribbean and an East Ender
My Sunday dinners include both roast potatoes and rice and peas
I can slip between BBC English, Cockney and Patois with ease
I relax with Jazz, dance to Hip Hop
Chill with Lovers but I love Bebop

You can't define me with a single entity
That's because I have a multiple identity
I'm not just multicultural
I'm also multiracial
I'm proud of my history and my roots
I dress, speak and communicate as it suits

You can't define me with just one word
To limit my multi culture would be absurd
The complexities
Of my multiple identities
Manifest in my eccentricities

They're wrapped up in my DNA, my blood, invasion, freedom
In Empire, enslavement, in race, belief, religion
In class and gender, language and dialect
Skills and talent, knowledge and intellect

Add to this the food I eat, the music I adore
The traditions I embrace and the passions I live for
If I am multicultural as I alone stand
I'm afraid Mr Prime Minister I don't understand

How you expect a whole population collectively
To be single cultured and have just one identity
And how you can believe multiculturalism's dead
When I'm a living legacy of its success

It's deep rooted, sometimes understated
Always there but never overrated
It's in the way we sing and the way we talk
The way we dance and the way we walk
Multiculturalism cannot fail to succeed
It's not in the gift of a politician to proceed
With its termination
It's not your creation

It's in our blood and in our bones
You can't create multicultural free zones
It's on our airwaves and in our streets
In our attire and rhythm and beats
It's in street food and haute cuisine
It's even in her majesty the Queen

It's in the theatre and in literature
In places of worship and Holy Scripture
Its celebration
Its jubilation
Its pomp and glory
And it's our story

You can't erase what makes us who we are
It's not something you can permit or bar
And you can't take away what brings us together
Recognise, Mr Prime Minister
Multiculturalism's here for ever. ❧

TRANSFORMATION

She was born out of devastation
Raised in destruction
Fed on deprivation
And nurtured with rejection

Blamed for existing
Punished for growing
Rejected for knowing
Abandoned for caring

Transformation was her only chance to survive
But first she had to recognise she was alive
Accept that she wasn't to blame
Sweep away the shame

Of first abuse, then neglect
Swallow pride and reject
But her emotions were intense
Her life made no sense

At first she wandered aimlessly
Each step taken painfully
Searching for answers to questions never asked
Trying to achieve actions not yet tasked

She bore her wounds and scars
Like glowing stars
Unashamed and defiant
Determined but quiet

Exposed her vulnerability
Because she didn't have the ability
To adapt to each social setting
Sinking into depression

When people turned away
In shock and dismay
Confused or embarrassed
Sometimes inexplicably astonished

She was like a warrior
And the rejection didn't worry her
Because she was used to being alone
Having to hold her own

But the expression in her eyes
Part angry, part crazy, part surprise
Told him she was on the edge
Hair dishevelled like an untrimmed hedge

But beyond her exterior
He saw she was far from inferior
Could see the beauty shining through
The tattered edges of her rue

At first she shunned his affections
Guarded against a history of rejections
Part curious, part bemused
And then tortured and confused

By the possibilities
And securities
That love might bring
And as she felt her heart sing

She collapsed under the weight
Of her changing fate
As she felt herself falling
She heard him calling

But failed to recognise her name
But who could blame
It had never been spoken
In the voice of tender men

In the moment that he caught her
It was like a supporting pillar
Had been removed from her spine
And the sensation was divine
It tantalised and tingled
Like tiny moonbeams sprinkled
Creating a warm glow around her heart
She clung to him like she never wanted to part

From the refreshing sensation
Of his intense attention
He carried her to a safe haven
Of hope and salvation
Slowly and steadily
She underwent readily
A transformation
Blossoming into creation

Of a strong sensitive
Loving, wanting to give
Pleased to receive
Ready to conceive

Human being
For the first time seeing
The undeniable beauty
Of love, guilt free

He witnessed her transformation
Eagerly without hesitation
He was painfully aware
So would not dare

To bask in the glory of it
He couldn't claim one bit
Because her transformation
Was not born from his invasion

Of her heart
He played no part
It was not because of his love but in spite
Because all she needed to feel alright

Was not to have his love - but the sensation of love itself.
In it she discovered a new found wealth
And made the transition from being alive to living
And embarked on her new beginning ❦

IN BLACK AND WHITE

Born of a two-fold nation
I caused quite a sensation
A mother black, a father white
I really was quite a sight

In sixties London it was rare
People passing stopped to stare

Black /White girl, Paki, Indian, Greek
Half caste, half pint and half breed

Why does your skin look so light?
How could your mum go with a white?
Why do you look like a parki?
Why did your dad go with a darky?

Half white, half black, 'half caste'
How long would this all last
I am a person, Whole! Complete!
A head! Two arms! Two legs! Two feet!

Born of a two-fold nation
It fills me with elation
A father white, a mother black
I'm me, I'm here and that's a fact

In nineties London it's not rare
And people do not stop and stare
African-Caribbean and Caucasian
Of mixed parentage, God's creation
A mother black, a father white
When will society see the light? ❧

Right to Vote

CHAPTER 4

WHAT HAPPENED YESTERDAY IMPACTS ON TOMORROW

Our beginnings, our pasts impact on our futures – if we don't know where we came from we can't know where we're going, experiences shape us - what doesn't break us only makes us stronger and so we learn, grow and shine.

WHAT DO YOU SEE?

When you look into the future, what do you see?
I see all races living in harmony....

I created a brand new being
So vulnerable, trusting and keen
The day that I gave birth
Was the day I felt self-worth
I truly prospered for the first time ever
When with the man I loved we created life together

But faced with the prospect of raising this beautiful child
I thought of the world outside and cried
I wanted a future for him where he would not have to fight
A world that would fill his soul with happiness and delight

If I wanted him to grow up positive and strong
I realised my present thinking was all wrong
I had to clear the bitterness I felt out of my mind
And leave the pain I had endured behind

I must instil within him his great value and worth
As a black male he has an important role upon this earth
He must be nurtured by the whole community
And if we hold strong he will be all he wishes to be

With strength and confidence of mind
He can leave the suffering of past generations behind
For these are millennium offspring hold the future in their hands
For they are the future leaders of our troubled lands

Let them not forget though, black or white
Our ancestors' sad and painful plight
And leave no question in their minds along the way
That black people have a valuable role to play
And in this country have every right to stay

When you look into the future, what do you see?
I see all races living in harmony

I see a land where people embrace their own cultures without
    living in fear
Where people respect each other and grow with love and care
A land where institutional racism is not tolerated
And the glass ceiling stopping our career progression has been
    eradicated

If we teach the youth while they are young
Let them know that they belong
If this is done by black and white alike
They'll grow to accept each other and unite

Only then can we bring a positive future into sight
And put the world right

When you look into the future what do you see?
I see all races living in harmony

I see my son fulfilling his potential
If we supply him with these ingredients that are essential
We'll raise a man whose view is balanced and is fair
I see a young man mentally and spiritually aware

If we work together for the future century
Our children can grow up to be exemplary

When you look into the future what do you see
I see all races living in harmony
Living in harmony ❧

NEW YEAR

It's something past midnight on New Year's Day morning
And as always a new day is dawning
Some people call it a new beginning
I can feel the old year thinning

'Last year' -words feel sweet on my lips
As I take tiny champagne sips
Don't really like champers but it's something we do
To ring out the old and welcome the new

Last year was a year of turmoil and grief
Where I often shed tears or kissed my teeth
But I need to remind myself of what I've accomplished
Because despite the downs I was truly blessed

I kept it real and represented
I persevered but never resented
Some days I was drowning but always survived
On making a difference my spirit thrived

I stood up, stood out
Didn't linger in doubt
My spirit may have scarred but was never broken
Because I always believed and kept my mind open

After sleep awoken on New Year's Day
By preachers who want to have their say
Awakening me to spread their word
But it's NEW YEARS - haven't they heard
My plan now awake - focus on the day ahead
Might as well get on since I'm out of bed
But I'll just stop on Facebook and have a cup of tea
How I change the world this year we'll just have to see

I know I can make a difference but I'd like to do more
Got to focus on what's at the core
New decade, New Year, new day
All things are possible if you find the way ❧

WOMAN IN THE MIRROR

I'd been let down so many times before
That I felt like I couldn't take it anymore
I started to believe there was something wrong with me
And that this was just the way it was going to be

Then one morning I awoke and I looked in the mirror
What I saw there filled me with terror
I shut my eyes and shook my head
Looked again and this woman looked back and said;

'Look at you, you're beautiful and kind
With a good heart and a strong mind
One day your time will come
And you'll meet that special someone
Just you wait and see
It'll set your heart free
Don't let other people's actions
Make you feel a lesser fraction
Of yourself – you are whole and complete
And one day you will meet
One who can appreciate your talents and strengths
Instead of indulging in jealousy and contempt'

I looked back at her and I said
I wish I could be more like you instead
You're in control and confident inside
I can't imagine you would ever hide
From the pressures of life
Getting dragged down, controlled by strife
She looked at me strangely
And then leaned into me
She had a sad look in her eyes
And what she said next took me by surprise

'Im just a mirror reflection
A visual interjection
What you see is just a facade
I can look soft or I can look hard
But you can go beyond an outer image
This is not where you finish
Step outside of your skin
Take a look at the you within
Because what's inside of you is real
I'm just a mirror image, that's the deal'

The years went passing me by
But whenever I felt like I wanted to die
I'd remember the mirror woman and what she said to me
Armed with new courage, I'd set my heart free
I'd step out of my skin
And look at the person within
Realise there was more I could be
Beyond what an eye could see
And it would set my heart free
To embrace the inner me ❧

RED, GOLD, GREEN AND SNOW

Days like this I feel I could stay inside forever
Protected from the snowy and stormy weather
Inhaling warm spices and fruit scented oil
Slowly letting the stresses of life uncoil

I could paint in red, gold and green while listening to Michelle
    Ndgeocello
Relax my mind, my mood chilled and mellow
Writing poetry on a cold winter afternoon
Wishing the summer would wrap its arms around me soon
But if I never went through life's challenges and strains
Or experienced its sorrow and pains
My pen and my brush would have no inspiration
And I'd have no need for relaxation

It's a harsh world but I've got a tough exterior
When others try to oppress I refuse to feel inferior
My life's been hard from birth to the present time
But I developed the determination to shine

I've never asked for favours or special treatment
Not allowed myself to be consumed by resentment
I don't have much, but what I have is a lot
I believe all things are possible, never say they're not

I've seen them materialise right before my eyes
But sometimes we all need to compromise
If the time isn't now doesn't mean it's never
And making sacrifices doesn't mean forever

I'm surrounded by the good and bad of people and nature
But I'm not just a doer, I'm a creator
I can conjure up a divine world or a story of gloom
Just with pens, paint and paper, here in my own front room

But I'd rather go out and experience the world
Even the days when abuse is hurled
This is what strengthens and shapes my existence
But just for today I'll opt for jazz, art and incense ✺

GLOBAL WARNING

Nature's wrath knows no limitation
If such anger was unleashed with intention
By humankind they'd call it abuse
But instead they put it on the news

Call it a *disaster*
Tut Tut that we didn't react faster
No court of human rights for Mother Nature
Whether you love her or hate her
She can launch a reign of terror
And never be penalised for her error
They say hell hath no fury like a woman scorned
This lady who's been globally warmed
By our pollution of her beautiful creations
Spares no man, woman or nations

Science and religion for once united in their prediction
Whilst successive governments debate jurisdiction
And the rumble of earth's belly
Is documented on the telly

But humans continue to ignore earth's global warning
Until they next time they hear Mother Nature's angry calling ❧

'Rise Up'
Acrylic & Ink on canvas

CHAPTER 5

SEEKING EQUALITY, FREEDOM, JUSTICE AND HUMANITY

Striving for equality, freedom, justice and humanity is not a choice but a necessity if we are to not just survive but live and thrive. Without equality there can be no freedom. Without freedom injustice remains. Without justice our rights as human beings are violated.

EQUALITY, FREEDOM, JUSTICE AND DEMOCRACY

Poets and griots for the truth searching
Through their words challenging and uplifting
Sharing our stories and their prediction
So I'll stand by my conviction
To inform and teach
Sometimes to preach
Striving for equality, freedom, justice and democracy
Some say it's a tall order for anybody
But if we all do our bit
Like pieces of a puzzle they'll fit
We'll see the full picture eventually
Understand this isn't an eccentricity

In my life they've been both strengthened and stripped away
So I have a duty every day
To protect these rights for my kin
Living without rights is like a sin
My resolve will never wear thin
I won't give up until I win
Fair and unbiased resolutions
That can bring about positive solutions

Every day our people are dying
See them on the news, we're not even crying
Forced labour and modern day slavery
Stripped of freedom and democracy
Don't think it can never happen to you
Because no one's immune no matter what you do
Too many believe such tragedy is what happens to others
Until it happens to their children, fathers or mothers
That's when they're fast tracked into activity
When once they were consumed by apathy

So by any communication means necessary
I'll use the power of word to express what matters to me
And I'll strive for Equality Freedom Justice and Democracy
Until death or eternity ❧

Part I

Equality

PROGRESSION

They're blocking me from progression
Trying to cause my regression
They can't abide
That I preside
Adept and articulate
Thinking *how ridiculous*
She's a woman, sole parent and black
We can't let her progress, not someone like that

I don't fit in with their Oxbridge ideal
I come from the streets, *I'm real*
I grew up in South London, Peckham
Raised by my Caribbean mum
I rate myself second to none

Not afraid to speak my mind
About discrimination I find
I know my rights and represent
All those people that they resent

They call me an *ethnic minority*
But not with my consent
I define myself as a **majority**
And that term they use I resent

*Only have to look at the world to see we make up the **majority***
That term is just mental slavery, designed to undermine the likes of
    you** and **me

So, they're blocking me from progression
Call it a permanent recession
Don't want someone of my gender or race
To honour their executive boards with my grace

But when I tell them how I feel
Give it to them straight, *remember I'm real*

They tell me they find me
Aggressive, confrontational and excessive
But you know if I was educated at Oxford, Cambridge or even Yale
They'd tell me they find me
Assertive, sensational and progressive

But I'm an ethnic **majority**
My ancestors fought slavery
And like a suffragette
It's not over yet
Because I'll rise above them one day soon
Despite their secret chants of the 'N' word and coon

You see I'm fired with a flame
That will burn out all their shame
I may not rise to fame
But I can play them at their own game
And though they won't give me a level playing field
To disseminate all I yield

Just remember I've combatted
Racism, sexism, fascism and oppression
Simultaneously, not in succession
And I'm still standing, still achieving
And there's no way I'm leaving

They may block my progression in the workplace
See this face
They may spit at it
Shut doors in it
Look down at it
Disregard it
But still I shine in the face of adversity
And I didn't need to go to university
To figure out
What they're about
I may be a woman and I may be black
But know something, I'm proud of that
Life isn't a concession

And I've got a confession
I overcame multiple oppression
So I sure as hell don't need permission
To achieve promotion or progression
And that's the end of this lesson. ❦

HIJABS AND HOODIES

Hijabs and hoodies
Deemed baddies not goodies
Blamed for society's ills
Justifying reason to kill

Looking for a scapegoat
Taking us by the throat
Or with the shot of a gun
No need after to hide or run

Because the law doesn't protect the victim
It defends them
The murderers and racists
Endorsing their hatred

Blame the hood, the cap
The locks, the hijab
The braids, the head wrap
The kufi, the turban
The scarf, the cornrows
The way your hair grows
But really it's about the race
The religion, the face
Of the person wearing
Not what they're wearing
Call it ignorance or fearing

But it's the hatred
Of being racist
Islamophobic
Xenophobic
Thinking that justifies
The theft of lives

Imagine if having your face
Meant your child wasn't safe
When they walked on the street
Fearful of whom they might meet

If buying a packet of candy from the store
Placed danger at their door
Imagine having to warn your child daily
Of the dangers that might be

Look out son for the EDL, the BNP
The police, the KKK
As you go on your way
Oh and generally crazed racists armed
With weapons to cause you harm

Bag of skittles, can of iced tea
Doesn't sound menacing to me
Beautiful face crowned by a warm hoodie

Could have been Obama's son, your son, my son
But he was the son of his pops and mom
Now shocked distraught grieving
Weeping, feeling
Hurt and dejected
Miserably failed and rejected
By a state, the law, the system
That doesn't protect the victim
But allows the perpetrator to claim self defence
Whilst the law accepts this pretence

And records the death of another beautiful bright young man
As a statistical faux pas - dusted and done
Their lives were precious, unique, special
Not another's to rule

Every young person with dreams and aspirations
Is someone else's inspiration
But to the authorities who treat them with disdain

They say they only had themselves to blame
It was the way they looked, spoke, dressed
That justified stabbing, shooting them in the head, the chest

Negative, racist, ignorant stereotyping
Which led to them lying there fighting
For one - last - breath - of - life - filled - air
Whilst snapshots of their time here

Flash before them signalling the end
For now they must transcend
Seeking peace in a better place
Whilst knowing it was just because of their race

That their life was stolen
And in that final moment
Praying that history will not repeat
And the good people will defeat

The evil of prejudice and racism
Stamp on the hatred of discrimination
Drive through justice
To replace the injustice

So now that's what we must do
Because if we don't it could be me or you
Next day, next month, next year
And the horror of that is too much to bear
It's time to rise, stand, mobilise
And whilst we dry our eyes

Of tears wept for lives taken
Whilst we feel our bodies shaking
Whilst our anger is raw and feelings bitter
We must remember we're better

Than those responsible for these crimes against humanity
Not allow our standards to be lowered by their profanity
Channel our anger into action and unity
Rise together with dignity

But determined resolve against the system
That allowed our loved ones to be labelled victim
Until we see justice is fully not partially served
And those responsible receive what they deserve ❧

TELL ME ABOUT RACISM

They tell me we're living in a post racial Britain
When the Government are undoing race laws written

They tell me Britain's a land of equal opportunity
Then in the same breath discriminate against me

They tell me I have a chip on my shoulder
Whilst they barricade doors with a heavy boulder

They tell me we have a very tolerant society
Then say they agree with the EDL and the BNP

They tell me that diversity's always embraced
Then tell me I don't fit in, I've got the wrong face

They tell me they're not racist, some of their best friends are black
Just before they embark on a verbal racist attack

They tell me I should be grateful to be living in the UK
And even though I'm born here, they still ask how long I'm
        planning to stay

They tell me they can't understand why there's a black history
        month
It's not like white people expect to have a white history month

They tell me you people are always wanting something more
Isn't it enough that Britain generously opened its door?

They tell me they're interested to know where I come from
Then go on to ask me if I've been here long

They tell me that political correctness has gone mad
Can't say anything for fear of offending, it's really sad

They tell me if we don't like it we can go back where we came from
If we weren't willing to fit in why did we come?

They tell me there's simply no racism here
So please can you stop your complaining dear

They tell me that it was nice to meet me
And they're sure now that I can see

That we're living in a post racial society
Blissfully unaware of their own hypocrisy ✣

BEING BLACK IS NOT A CRIME

Black lives are still treated with less worth
Like we don't have an equal role on earth
White privilege wielding power over black lives
Like we don't have entitlement to the same rights

Police shoot not to apprehend but to kill
They won't stop until they've had their fill
Of red blood from black bodies shed
Yes just like them, we bleed red

Yet still perceived as the other
Whilst police hide under cover
Of carrying out their lawful duty
Whilst politicians act as trial and jury

Debating us but not including us
On our tel-lie-visions they discuss
As if we are a problem that has to be solved
Like we're a separate species that hasn't evolved

Rather than focusing on the real perpetrators of crime
Those who act as though taking black lives is a pastime
Those who judge us whilst defending the police
Those who witness the murder of our kin with ease

Then fail to acknowledge the reason for our anger
Using terms to describe us like looter or rioter
Refusing to see the mother crying in despair
The father trying to raise his sons with care

The sister mourning the loss of her brother
The frightened young man labelled 'the other'
Martin Luther King said 'a riot is the language of the unheard'
Decades of debate, policy, laws – and they haven't heard a word

As if having a black president in the USA
Compensates the racism we experience today
Or cancels out the racism we faced historically
Or erases our experience of its legacy

Over 50 years since the civil rights movement was born
And we're still waiting, still fighting for a new dawn
Where black lives are not deemed as cheap
But the root of racism runs deep

From enslavement to colonial rule
Systems of power, hateful and cruel
Apartheid and segregation
Abuse, blocking our emancipation

We've had to raise our children to fight
So what gives police the right
To take lives with a shot of a gun
Once fired it can't be undone

There can be no level of remorse
No government proposed recourse
That can bring back the stolen lives of our kin
Taken just because of the colour of skin

Every aspect of life, day and night
We're forced to stand up for our right
To live with dignity and equality
As strong as we have been forced to be

We should not have to teach our youth
About this frightening and painful truth
Or what to do when an officer's in pursuit
Where do we go when even with hands up shouting don't shoot
Police are empowered and backed by systems
That see us as guilty even though we're the victims
What we are experiencing is systemic
This is a racism epidemic

If after centuries of murder and abuse
The powers that be still refuse
We have no choice but to rise up angry and outraged
2014 and they think it's okay to have black people caged

City of London labels it art, claims it will be an education
As if we need a lesson on race discrimination
As if racists will change their minds by the re-enactment
All this serves to do is humiliate us for their enjoyment

Whilst subjecting us to more oppression
This isn't art, its degradation
If they want to challenge racism for real
Stop subjecting us to this nightmare ordeal
Stop killing our children, end deprivation
Tackle the root causes of under representation
We will not be silenced by oppression
But don't get it twisted, that isn't aggression

It's called strength and determination
As we strive each day for full emancipation
Whilst our babies are murdered we won't stand back
Until people recognise that it's not a crime to be black ❧

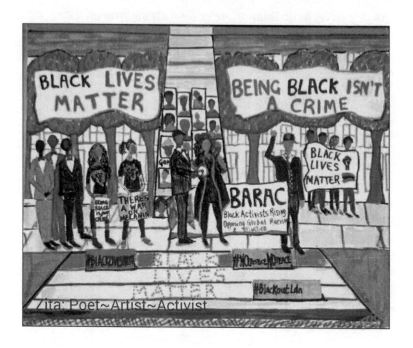

'Black Lives Matter'
Ink on Acrylic

SAY MY NAME WHEN I WIN OLYMPIC GOLD

F*****g N****r when I'm suspected of a crime
Black monkey when I'm doing time
Dirty N*g N*g when I marry your relation
Seeking special treatment when I challenge discrimination
Immigrant in times of recession
Asylum seeker when I'm escaping persecution
Aggressive when I stand up for my rights
Suspect if I'm out late at night
Jamaican if I'm playing loud music
Ethnic Minority when I'm a statistic
Suspected terrorist if I'm dressed traditionally
Happy clappy if I practice Christianity
Fanatic if I'm of any other religion
Migrant if I'm second generation
Gang member if I'm in a group of more than three
Thug if I'm dressed in a hoodie
Foreigner if I'm bilingual
Failing to assimilate if I'm unique and individual
Scrounger if I live in social housing
Wannabe if I try conforming
Monkey if you stop and search me
Lying W*g if you and I don't agree
Savage if I'm observing a family tradition
Extremist if I'm subjected to extradition
Representing the UK if I'm playing professional sport
Suspected drug dealer as I return from holiday at the airport
Overstayed my welcome when I'm growing old
But I become British when I win Olympic Gold

Every day I'm labelled as my true story goes untold
You only say my birth name when I win Olympic Gold 🏃

Part II
Freedom

THRESHOLD TO FREEDOM

It was cold, she was tired, drained of strength
But she knew they'd go to any length
It was now or never to get away
If she wanted to live to see another day

She crept slowly in stages, listening
Fearful, she felt the sweat glistening
She unlatched the door slowly
Hand shaking, dropped the key

She froze in the pitch dark
In the distance heard a dog bark
Instinctively cowered, head under arm
Shielding herself from anticipated harm

Slowly she patted her palm on the ground
Breathed a silent sigh when the key was found
Placed this symbol of freedom in the lock
Heart beating loud as a ticking clock

Pushed down the handle quiet as a mouse
Prayed she'd never again enter this house
As it opened, the door creaked loudly in the night
Something, perhaps a mouse, scuttled away in fright

In her rush to cross the threshold of freedom she stumbled
Adrenaline pumping, nervously she giggled
Fear and excitement rolled into a single emotion
So long a victim of oppression

She half fell, half crawled over the threshold
And in that moment she felt brave and bold
Straightened up her bruised and broken body
And shook off the invisible chains of slavery

Renewed energy, she fled into the night air
Guided by the stars, wind in her hair
She ran until she reached a place of safety
And wept tears of joy knowing she was free. ❧

I DIED A MILLION TIMES FOR MY FREEDOM

My Freedom was not gained in a day, a month or a year
To achieve it I had to overcome both sorrow and fear
I walked across continents and centuries
Many times stumbling, falling down on my knees

I died a million times for my Freedom

Not a day passed when I wasn't grieving
But I never gave up, never stopped believing
That I would reach the destination called Freedom
Sometimes I cried for my Freedom

Other times I died for my Freedom
My body and soul became my own Queendom
The ground beneath my feet never there long enough to call home
Constantly I ventured to uninviting pastures unknown

I died a million times for my Freedom

Be it one century or one year
I could sense Freedom always near
The scent of sweet liberty permeated my nostrils
I etched songs of Freedom in my mind that became my gospels
Strong and defiant, never forgetting proud roots
Passed through DNA to my womb's precious fruits

I died a million times for my Freedom

Sometimes I was taken, sometimes I was used
Other times I was tortured and abused
My tears of sorrow deepened the sea
Broadening the divide between Freedom and me

Rebellion gave me hope and determination
My resistance knew no boundary or limitation
I bore the scars of my captivity
Like tribal marks of identity

I died a million times for my Freedom

When I was held back physically
I charted the route to Freedom mentally
In order to keep journeying towards my goal
The map of Freedom was imprinted on my soul

Between the stench of bodies decayed
And so many promised loyalties betrayed
I caught fast breaths of sweet fresh air
I could taste Freedom drawing near

I died a million times for my Freedom

When I couldn't run I walked
When I couldn't walk I talked
Promoting the very concept of Freedom to all who would hear
Convinced that Freedom could be reality if only they would dare

To claim it as their right
They could bring it into sight
When I could no longer walk, I rested
Learning that if I invested

In my own physical and mental well being
I would never stop believing
That Freedom could be mine
And when I finally arrived the sensation was divine

I died a million times for my Freedom

Even though I was wearied by centuries of oppression
Aged beyond my years by sadness and depression
Weathered from exposure to extreme elements
Frail from multiple abuses and resentments

I embraced my Freedom like an old lost friend
And refused to release my grasp for fear it would end
I died a million times for my Freedom
I died a million times for my Freedom
I died a million times for my Freedom ❧

SAFE HAVEN

In my mind I travel to safe havens and treasured retreats
Savouring memories like the first taste of special treats
Sweet fresh air like the scent of freshly laundered sheets
Warmth on my face from the midday rays as sun beats

My journey is not easy, I stumble some and fall
Sometimes I hear the beckoning of an evil spirit call
But each time I rise up, dust myself down, stand tall
Then run to my destiny along this never ending hall

I gather strength held in the deep hidden blue
Listen, look, feel for the next golden clue
That will lead me on my way, tell me what to do
Take me to the place where I can feel brand new

It's a challenge to progress as I travel on
Difficult sometimes to know right from wrong
To keep my spirits up I sing a familiar song
Take comfort in the lyrics when the melody's gone

I witness sadness, pain and encounter dangers
Never knowing whether to trust the kindness of strangers
Some I hear whispering 'we just want to change her'
Others who just want to detain and deter

Obstacles and barriers placed right in my way
Beckoning to me to give up, surrender, and stay
Blocking me, hoping where I fall I will lay
Never rising to see or live another day

But the sensation of my safe haven beckons me
This is the place where I can truly be free
This is the place where I can simply be
So I know that I must complete this journey ❧

Part III
Justice

STRANGE KIND OF JUSTICE

In memory of Stephen Lawrence

Strange kind of justice
That takes a life of 18 years and takes 18 years more to serve
Where only some of the guilty get the punishment they deserve

Strange kind of justice
That can allow killers to grow freely into adulthood
Yet deprive that of the bright, beautiful young man they brutally took

Strange kind of justice
That allows racism to thrive even though it's against the law
That supports a judicial system that's rotten to the core

Strange kind of justice
That regards some lives as cheaper and more inferior than others
And allows the innocent to live in anguish and suffer

Strange kind of justice
That allows the injustice of murder and prejudice to thrive
And keeps the ignorance of discrimination alive

Strange kind of justice
That leaves mothers, fathers, families, communities in pain
That dares to take the names of equity and liberty in vain

Strange kind of justice
That looks on with disinterest whilst families fight for a lifetime
Whilst the guilty unremorseful and defiant are given a lifeline

Strange kind of justice
That offers a distorted, biased imbalance of scales
Tilted to keep murderers and racists away from the jails

Strange kind of justice
That sees a police force cast aside facts and evidence
Disregarding human rights along with reason and sense

Strange kind of justice
That requires wealth and power in order to be accessed
That shuts its doors on the least empowered and the poorest

Strange kind of justice
That would see a mother set aside her right to grieve
Forced to challenge all those that failed her and dared to deceive

Strange kind of justice
That would take credit for a family's perseverance and tenacity and
    dare to celebrate
When it eventually and only partially delivered eighteen sad and
    painful years too late ❧

UPRISING

On the streets of Tottenham flames ignite
Frustrations explode and the press call it 'riot'
Our lives are cheap in the eyes of the police
Protected by those who don't want us to have peace
Government claim it's unacceptable
Their condemnation is predictable
The revolution will not be televised
Because the BBC have to take cover and hide
Politicians and pundits demonising our youth
Refusing to acknowledge the plain and simple truth
That poverty, deprivation and injustice are at the root
I hear the cry of anguish of those pursuing loot
They're not thugs or loutish or driven by greed
When government and police refuse to heed
The pain and anger - signs and words of warning
They should have predicted the days of unrest dawning
When you take away the means to get an education
Destroy the aspirations and hopes of a generation
Take away lives and deny people justice
Impose policies that are unfair and racist
Take away opportunity and bar access to progress
You can't expect silence whilst you oppress
An uprising is a cry for help, for change, for people to listen
The way to respond is not to instigate division
Isolating our young
Labelling them as wrong
If you refuse to acknowledge and do what's right
There'll be no calm on our streets at night
Until you mend what's broken in the system
Address the root not punish the victim
You must eliminate poverty and discrimination
Take responsibility for the devastation
Created not by youth but by bankers and tax dodgers
Target the real economic and social destroyers ✣

BLOOD STAINED GOLD

For the miners and families of South Africa seeking justice for silicosis

Golden gold
Story untold
Stolen by white gold diggers
Abusing black gold workers
Diseasing their lungs
Failing to correct their wrongs

So that golden gold turns red
Stained with the blood of those now dead
Black workers treated like slaves
Forced to mine the deepest caves
In order to earn one or two rand
Prisoners in their own land

Whilst their oppressors
Are now the possessors
Of multi-national companies
Feasting on the profits of their slavery
Stolen gold from a stolen land
Now refusing a helping hand

For families dying from poverty
Whilst they live in luxury
Thriving on the wicked legacy of apartheid
This isn't a matter of taking sides
In the years that justice has been sought
Thousands more have been caught

By this harsh reality and lost their lives
Leaving behind children, parents, wives
Too poor to live, too abandoned to die
And whilst their children cry
From pains of hunger
They're too fatigued for anger

Those mines stole their lives
Cut up their lungs like knives
Whilst in Western countries
Working class communities
Sell their gold jewels by the gram
To 'scrap' gold buyers who don't give a damn

Grabbing the opportunity to profit more
Eager to exploit this new Western poor
Forced to sell the blood stained golds
Whilst their own misery unfolds
Caught in the misfortune of economic downturn
Whilst bankers and government leaders still earn

More in a week than poor people do in years
And for each pound they earn black miners shed as many tears
And the same ones who melt down symbols of milestones
Offer at the same time they take the lure of 'no pay day' loans
Exchanging pennies for gold, greedy for more
To benefit the rich who stole the red stained stolen ore

Over indulged in sugary delights molars bleed
And are swapped with gold to rectify their sugar feed
Bodies adorned with red and white gold to wipe away the blues
Whilst multi-national companies refuse
To provide compensation and medical care
To those they abused for decades not years

Gold -the stuff of fairy tales and broken dreams
Mythology, movies and midday sun beams
Golden rings to seal wedding day vows
But no one stopped to ask the whens, wheres and hows
Polishing each golden treasure until it glows
But over time the blood stain grows

Dulling the allure of the precious metal
As each dying worker drops like the petal
Of a single rose in cellophane wrap on Valentine's Day
Beaus anxious that 'I do' are the words their lovers will say

And their proposals come with bands of stolen golds
Garnished with stolen blood diamonds and emeralds
And still the story goes untold of how the worshipped metal held
in such high esteem
Made its journey through oppression and racism to feed the cat
that got the cream
It's said that all that glitters is not gold but all that's gold does not
glitter
Or the preciousness and value of the over worked and under paid
miner
Would have been honoured and recognised
Not disregarded and compromised
In a quest for riches at the expense of humanity
This is the harsh callous reality

Even the gold didn't escape segregation

White gold, red gold, yellow gold, black gold
Each piece with a story untold
Black gold stained with red blood stolen by white gold thieves
Who thrive on yellow gold dreams while the black gold miner
grieves

Blood Stained Gold ❧

THE INJUSTICE OF JUSTICE; EXTRADITION

She was born in the land of the ancestors, raised in the city of Angels, lived her early adult life on an island made of dreams, pursued by a government intent on dominating the world, imprisoned in a jail situated on stolen land, tried in a court room built on the backs of enslaved peoples torn from the land of the ancestors that was her birth.

She was deemed guilty until proven innocent, labelled before they knew her name, persecuted with no crime to charge her for, taken despite refusing to surrender her freedom, demonised because of her religion, misunderstood because of her multicultural upbringing, rejected because of her ancestry, disregarded as a human being and seen to be entitled to no rights upon this earth.

She refused to break when they tortured her, denied them the pleasure of seeing her weep when her heart was breaking, refused to let them see her turning crazy when she felt herself losing her mind, between the beatings, as she lay in solitary confinement for days that were the same as nights, , she comforted herself with the recollection of words spoken by great philosophers and poets and memorised verses created out of the depths of her soul about the injustice of justice, remained resilient, determined and brave, held on to her belief that the truth would one day set her free because she'd been raised to value her worth. ❧

Part IV
Humanity

HER NAME

They are human - being
Breathing, hearing, seeing
Hoping to find their way
To keep danger at bay

Caused by Western intervention
It had never been their intention
To leave beloved homes and flee
Separated from loved ones and family

No time to think of the perils and danger
Placing not just trust but future in a stranger
Survival instinct now just to stay alive
Praying for a way when they arrive

It took courage to get to this stage
Huddled, listening to the storm rage
Monster waves on an unknown sea
Rocking them from side to side angrily

Drifting into an uneasy sleep
She could still hear them weep
Tears of sorrow for all they'd lost
Tears of pain for the human cost

It was sudden and brutal
The sea so ice cold cruel
She tried to cling on to humanity
Willing herself, desperately …

But now she's just a number
Here in her eternal slumber
They can't hear her scream
I had hopes, a dream

I was a human being
With emotion and feeling
I had aspirations and goals
I fulfilled many roles

I was a daughter and a mother
A wife, a protector, a lover
I was an artist, a creator
A writer and a narrator

I told stories of old
Painted tales in gold
I came from a great ancestral line
Passion, desire, love were mine

I embraced ancient traditions
Whilst having future ambitions
I nurtured the young and soothed the old
Made sure our story didn't go untold

Like many others I was wounded, persecuted
A victim of war, tortured and exploited
I lost my home, my job, my kin
It was a battle I could not win

Now you describe me as a recovered body
Not a human being, not a somebody
At best I am just anybody
At worse I am a nobody

You describe me as a would be immigrant
Not a woman, a mother, just a migrant
At best I am just one of the dead
At worse I am simply deceased instead

Some describe me as an African
That their countries planned to ban
Did you know that Africa is a continent?
Isn't my country of birth important?

Some call me a refugee
A victim of a manmade tragedy
That drowned in the sea
Describe me statistically

Some of you think I am lesser than human
Genderless, I'm not even a woman
Describing me as an insect, a pest
As though I was coming to infest

My life that was, now part of a death toll
Like I wasn't an individual with a role
At worse one of the thousands drowned
At best one of the bodies found

But if they didn't hear her screams in life
When her husband's throat was slit with a knife
If they didn't hear her screams when she was raped
Or when she fled in the night, escaped

If they didn't hear her screams of hunger
When she sobbed tears of pain and anger
If they didn't hear her screams in the sea
As she waved her hands desperately

If they didn't hear her screaming then
Her tortured soul wonders if and when
They will come to realise she isn't just a number
Her name is all she wants them to remember ❧

BULLINGDON GANGSTER

Born rich, yet still you were a gang member
Grew up in luxury but that didn't curb your temper
You never experienced destitution
Yet still ended up in an institution

With your gang lashing out
Acting like a thug and lout
Destroying properties just for fun
Showing no remorse for what you'd done

You said you did things when you were young
That you believe you shouldn't have done
But still you managed to escape the judicial system
Each time throwing money to bribe your victim

Drinking, vomiting on and trashing property
But not as a response to extreme poverty
You said the riots are about a culture that disrespects authority
Drawing on your own failure to act properly

You said the parents of these children don't care who they're with
I wonder after your parents found out who you were with
They were able to forgive?
Hanging around with fellow thugs of your Bullingdon Gang
Did they discipline you or forbid you to hang

With other members of your gangster paradise
Destroying businesses before the owners' eyes
Perhaps as you escaped punishment at the time
You should be evicted from No.10 for your crime

Perhaps you ought to practice what you preach and receive a
        prison sentence
Pledge your remorse and demonstrate your repentance
You stated that children today end up in gangs through neglect
Shame on your parents that your childhood was wrecked

Perhaps if your parents had kept you at home
Instead of forcing you to live alone
You wouldn't have committed the violent crimes you did
Then when the police came ran away and hid

It seems your bad upbringing led to a life of stealing
Taking taxpayers money for your conservatory roof resealing
And other property repairs which you agreed to repay
Yet you continued thieving public sector pensions and pay

Your lack of respect for family values
And failure to collect revenues
Has led to many of your friends committing crime
Avoiding and failing to pay their taxes on time

This has led to parents of the children you despise
Having to work two or three jobs just to survive
You've been taxing the poor
To pay the rich more

So Mr Prime Minister when you talk about breaking the law
Perhaps you need to look first to your own front door ✨

WHAT KIND OF WORLD IS THIS?

What kind of world is this where those supposed to uphold the law
Break it with impunity, take lives like they matter no more
Empowered by institutions, stained with the blood of black women
    and men
Unwavering in their hatred even when taking the lives of children

What kind of world is this where 'black lives matter' is a hashtag
Where a trip to the shop could end in a body bag
Where 'hands up don't shoot' is a protest slogan
Held up in response to black lives stolen

What kind of world is this where the systemic denigration
Oppression, race and sex discrimination
Pervading every element of life and society
Denies the right in life to dignity and equity

But is also structured to protect the perpetrators
When lives are brutally taken, appointing infiltrators
To obstruct the course of justice, distorting truths as they spy
On families too tortured by their quest for truth to even cry?

What Kind Of World Is This? ❦

THIS IS NOT THE GREAT AMERICAN DREAM

Children begging on the street
Walking with no shoes upon their feet
Collecting tin cans, playing on railway tracks
Searching through rubbish bins in search of scraps

THIS IS NOT THE GREAT AMERICAN DREAM

Mothers unable to put meals on tables
Carrying the stigma of pointed fingers and labels
Redundancy leading to homelessness
Destitute and feeling helpless

THIS IS NOT THE GREAT AMERICAN DREAM

Families of 5, 6, 7 or 8 living in one room
Praying for a miracle to come one day soon
Riddled with vermin, overcrowded
Either frowned upon or disregarded

THIS IS NOT THE GREAT AMERICAN DREAM

Living off cans of salt water vegetables and beans
Treated like inferior worthless human beings
Dependent on food banks where a can of spam's a luxury
Consigned to a lifetime of isolation and poverty

THIS IS NOT THE GREAT AMERICAN DREAM

Evicted with less than twenty four hours to pack
Told you're only allowed what you can fit in one sack
Moving from homeless shelter to motel to cardboard box
Knowing the only education they'll get is at the school of hard
    knocks

THIS IS NOT THE GREAT AMERICAN DREAM

This is the reality for children in the world's richest nation
Where millions of children are in this preventable situation
Barred from healthcare, education and security
Reducing their life chances to a future of poverty

MR PRESIDENT;
 THIS IS NOT THE GREAT AMERICAN DREAM ❧

Our Struggles are Connected

CHAPTER 6

RESISTANCE

Resistance is necessary in order to bring about positive change. With courage and determination we can be the inspiration we seek and the change we desire.

RESIST AND RISE

We're living in a Con-Dem nation
Fighting for emancipation
They're ripping the clothes off our backs
In just one more attack upon attacks
Cutting our jobs, our services, our means of living
Relentless, but expecting us to be understanding
Cutting the heart out of our community
Acting without humanity

No step on the ladder
Struggling just for bread and butter
If we don't fight back we'll end up in the gutter
Feel like screaming at them but they'll call me a nutter
Cart me away in a straitjacket with flashing lights
To a place where days are the same as nights
Throw away the key because of funding cuts
React with disapproval and tut tuts
Regard me as a burden on society
Blame me for the state of the economy
Place me in solitary confinement, turn out the lights
Strip me of my dignity and all my rights

Rights that were fought for from generation to generation
Damn this Con-Dem nation
While the poor get poorer the rich run government
But now's not the time to wallow in pity and resentment

Time to resist
Persist
Insist
On justice, equality
Fairness and equity
Words that politicians bounce around
Like surround sound
Never digesting their meaning
Even if they purport to have a left leaning

Time to rise
Get wise
Organise

If not it's the start of our demise
Time to stamp on their spin and lies
Open up our minds and eyes
Pretending it's not happening and not engaging
Won't erase the reality of what we're facing
We must resist and rise
Be strong and wise
Have to rise and resist
Demand and insist
Need to resist and rise
Campaign and organise
No choice but to rise and resist
Focus and persist

Resist and Rise
Resist and Rise
Resist and Rise ⚘

MARCH 26TH MARCH

On coaches and trains from all parts of UK
They assembled on Embankment to have their say
To send a clear message to the government of the day
That they were not giving up or going away

Some marched, some orated
Some stamped on the hatred
Some acted defiant
But not were complacent

Some placards were donated
Some lovingly created
Some held banners high
Some waved flags to the sky

Many marchers felt cheated
Refusing to be defeated
Some meeted and greeted
A few were VIP treated

Some were with family
All were in unity
Some made a new friend
All prepared to defend

Some rose up early, travelled by night
One walked to march through a week of daylight
There were children and elders
Trade unions and workers

Some voiced for the voiceless
Some marched for the powerless
Some were quiet, some were loud
Some were out and proud

There were black activists rising
Disabled groups leading
Women blocks of purple and green
Bold and bright so they'd be seen

Some were on foot, some on shoulders
Some were four legged, some carried banners
Some came in wheelchairs
Some came with pushchairs

Some were civil servants, some fire fighters
Some nurses and carers, some were bus drivers
Some had flags, some placards displayed
Holding up inflatables whilst hands were waved

Some were worshippers, some were atheists
Some were politicians, some were socialists
Some were students and some were teachers
Some were dressed up like very strange creatures

Some took direct actions
Some were in factions
Some proudly displayed trade union names
Some came from local or national campaigns

Some marched into Hyde Park
Some stayed way after dark
Some sheltered a while to avoid the rain
Some left early to catch a bus or train

Some marched for education and job security
Some marched for freedom and democracy
Some marched for justice, some against poverty
Some marched against discrimination and for equality

Some went on to rally at Trafalgar Square
Until the police arrived with their riot gear
Five Hundred Thousand marched for the alternative
On the March 26th March, strong, determined and positive. ❧

AFTER THE MARCH IS DONE

One day united in pain, anger, sorrow
But when it comes to tomorrow
And you've gone your separate ways
Filling up your regular days
With life's daily responsibilities and pressure
When you're spending time at your leisure

Will you remember when we were strong and united
Flames of emotion ignited
Ready to take action come what may
Do you dream at night of revolution on the way

After the march is done
Will you carry on?

Different reasons brought us there
Some came weighted with a pain too heavy to bear
Some came to holler and cheer
Some came out of anger or fear
Some came to make history
Some came expecting victory

Young ones were brought to learn and know
Some came so that they could show
Their organisations solidarity
Some to provide a link in a chain of unity

Peaceful, sad, jubilant, strong
Marching, marching, marching along
Answers, justice and change all sought
Abstract treasures that can't be bought
Departing with a handful of determination and a heart full of hope
When you got home did you still feel equipped to cope?

After the march is done
Will you carry on?

With the responsibility of making a stand
Did you know where to reach out for a helping hand
Are you ready to be a strong link
In a volatile chain on the brink
Or are you satisfied to reminisce the day
With photos and videos on display

Do you burn with a hunger stronger than the pain we have endured
Are you ready to rise up, raise your voice, be seen and heard
Are you prepared to sacrifice some daily pleasures
Take the necessary measures

Be a foot soldier one day, a leader another
Make the revolution your significant other

After the march is done
Will you carry on?

Or will you smile and nod at the footage on TV
Pat yourself on the back and say 'that was me'

Feeling self- satisfied that you were there
What's holding you back, is it apathy or fear
Or worse are you resigned to a fate
Where power is taken by those that hate
Unable to carve a path of self- empowerment
Wearied by bitterness and resentment

Anger can be channelled into positive energy
If you allow yourself to be in synergy
With those who share the same desire and aspiration
Of a different world free of oppression

Where law is not allowed to be misused
And power isn't taken and abused
Where the judicial system
Doesn't side against the victim
Where justice gets served
And our oppressors get what they deserve

All of this is possible
If we dare to dream the impossible
If we assert our power collectively
Stand up as one in unity

So when the march is done
Remember we've only just begun
Your role is not complete
Until we defeat
And our right to humanity is addressed
Until we cease to be oppressed
So after the march is done
Doesn't mean we've won
Doesn't mean your support's no longer required
And even though you may be tired

Your contribution is still needed
Because power isn't conceded
Without the determination of demand
At all times we must be armed
With the power of the collective
So don't stand back and be selective

About when and how you participate
After the march is done don't deviate
After the march is done carry on
Stay until the battle's won
Stay after the march is done

After the march is done
We must all carry on
When you think there's nothing left to do
We are all still in need of you ❧

UNTIL THE FAR RIGHT ARE HISTORY

My life's been peppered, sometimes drenched in racist attacks
My family came here to signs of 'no dogs, no Irish, no blacks'
I grew up with racist abuse hurled in glee
Words that like a suture cut into me

So now I have a responsibility
And the strength and ability
To stand up, fight and defend
Until we see an end

My mental scars won't deter
I won't be fearful of what might occur
Can't sit back and let history repeat
Got to stand up and defeat

Whilst I'm living and breathing
I'll never stop believing
That we can beat the far right
We can if all good people unite

Until there's no racist on my ballot form
Until people accept fascism's not the norm
Until there are no far right on the street
Until we truly defeat
We've got to act urgently
There's no room for complacency
Until the far right are history
And we truly have victory ✺

NEW YEAR SAME BLUES

New Year, same blues
Live or die, choose
New Year, same battle
Still swimming upstream without a paddle

Still facing hardship and discrimination
Still ruling our lands as an institution
Dictating how the poorest should live
Only willing to take, never to give
Every day's a battle for survival
Fighting back, striving for a revival

Of people power and equality
Even though I'm not afraid to just be me
I'm still striving for the day when I'm free
New Year, same reality
Still standing up against brutality

Either punished for breathing
Or penalised for believing
Sometimes targeted, sometimes shunned
Often shocked but never stunned
Because my motto is to keep on keeping on
Challenge all I experience that's wrong

Determined to succeed and do what's right
Life should be for living not a fight
I won't rest until justice is in sight
New Year, same resolution
I won't rest until there's a solution

For all who have suffered the worse of humanity
Living on the edge of insanity
Whilst the arrogant and rich make rash decisions
Wounding us as they do with exact incisions
Aimed at harming the most vulnerable
Viewing them as undesirable

Disregarding the fact that they're human too
Treating them like animals in a zoo
Ridiculing them in their sorrow and rue
New Year, another day
Of hurdles and barriers blocking my way

Life is hard but I have to be tough
Less than nothing isn't enough
I worked too long and hard for gain
To give up and surrender for my pain
Try to wake up those sleeping in my midst
Make them realise that we need to resist

People if we don't unite it will be our demise
If you've one New Year resolution, open up your eyes
And make it be to stand up and rise

New Year, same blues
Live or die, choose

New Year, same rain
Dampened spirits, raw pain
New Year, same blues ♭♮

'*Embracing Me*'
Acrylic on paper

CHAPTER 7

EMOTIONAL EXPRESSIONS; DAILY REFLECTIONS

Expressing how we feel is healing - healing is necessary in order to grow mentally and spiritually so that we don't just survive but blossom, thrive and live.

ALL I CAN BE

I am
I am all
I am all I can be
I am all I can be at any given time
In all I do I aspire to shine
Blending words with people, causes and art
Sometimes alone but always a part
Of something bigger striving for more
Searching for what's at the core
Seeking equality, freedom, justice and humanity
Always looking forward but grounded in my history
Fighting for my rights, your rights, every day
I stand up to those who get in the way
Of justice and equity
I don't give up easily
Spiritual kin call me a griot of the struggle
Those who feel threatened tag me maker of trouble
I reject the labels and stereotypes they try to pin to me
Refuse to be intimidated, express myself freely
I am words, I am feelings, I am expressions
Embracing spirituality not possessions
I am colour, I am imagery, I am vision
Striving for fulfilment not position
I am comfortable in my own skin
I have no desire to conform or fit in
In all I do I aspire to shine
I am all I can be at any given time
I am all I can be
I am all
I am ❧

ONE MORE TEAR

As one more tear drops from my eye
I try so hard not to cry
Just one solitary crystal tear
But still it's more than I can bear

I catch it in my open palm

In a blink of my eyes
I'm able to symbolise
All of my fears and sorrow
To tender to think of tomorrow
My life is deteriorating
And here I am creating
On more solitary tear
As if it can calm my fear

My face used to shine
With laughter that was all mine
But now I only snatch at others' happiness
Like an uninvited guest
Seems like another lifetime
Since I tasted the divine
All that I have left
Is the bitter bile of contempt

Blinking back
My eyelash flaps
Soaked in the salt of pure crystal tears
That holds the bitter memories of many years
And as one more tear drops from my eye
I swear I'm not going to cry
Anymore, I'm all cried out
And there's more to living than sorrow and doubt ❧

SILENT STRENGTH

Some strength you cannot see
It's the kind of strength that will always be
Slowly growing
Glowing
Proud but not boastful
Determined and hopeful
Developed out of a history of oppression
Progressed against attacks and division
Quiet but sure
Loving and pure
Created out of a need to survive
To breathe and stay alive
Blossoming
Progressing
Never digressing
An open lesson
Strength that created new life even whilst enslaved
Strength that walked over the fresh soil of its own grave
And said no to surrender and death
Exhaled even with its last breath
Strength that found freedom even whilst it was still chained
Strength that cannot be touched, defined or named
Strength that risked all it had to give freedom to others
Strength that unlocks, releases, uncovers
The true art of embracing life even when everything has gone
Continues to thrive when all else is shrivelled and done
Strength that seeks no thanks or praise
Strength that breaks through barriers and finds ways
To grow, blossom
Smile, listen
Share
Hear
Feel
Heal
Even when it feels like falling
It hears a silent calling

And gathers up every entity
Of its identity
To embrace courage
Unite and encourage
All around to have a chance
To enhance
Or accept
And even when all that could be is wrong
To remain resilient and strong ❧

THANK MUSIC I'M ALIVE

Songs, melodies, rhythms - the sound track
Of every step, breath, embrace, attack
Of my life, my years
My laughter, my tears
One line of one song
Can whisk me along
To a time, a place
A safe space
A horrible memory
An enemy
Each intricate moment of my existence
Brought to the forefront of my mind intense
Every detail, emotion
The song is like a magic potion
Conjuring up a memory
In an instant sent to me
Through a beautiful melody
And in a second
I ascend
And land
And in my mind
Is an episode
Feel like I'll explode
If I can't go back to that time
To a moment that was divine
Or full of sorrow
Where I longed for a new tomorrow
But even when things were tough
Even when I'd had enough
There was always a song
To carry me along
Lift me up, dry my tears
Documenting the years
Of my journey
Always dear to me

Without my total love of music I sometimes believed I could not
survive
It's thanks to beats, rhymes, riffs, rhythms, melodies and lyrics that
I'm alive ❧

FIVE MINUTES

Five minutes alone to think
Saves me perching on the brink
Of anger and insanity
Gives me the opportunity
To reflect and breathe
Give thanks I'm able to achieve
Appreciate where I've come from
What still needs to be done
Give thanks I'm still standing
Still living, still loving
Smile for the beauty that surrounds me
Cry for the hatred that invades me
Gather strength and determination
To fight for the next generation
Against the attacks they face
Strive for them to see better days
Appreciate my role as a mother
A giver, carer and nurturer
Feel blessed that I'm able to share my gift
To spread knowledge and uplift
Five minutes alone
Enough to keep me going ✿

THE SHINE THAT BRIGHTENS UP YOUR DAYS

I am the colour of ripened fruit
As strong as an ancient tree root
No boundaries can hold me back
In boldness I do not lack

Some say my eyes have yellowed
But I am bold, not mellowed
I am golden & sweet juice
My intention is not just to seduce

But for you to see yourself in me
To a lesser or fuller degree
I am enriched tones
Glowing through my structured bones

I have no beginning and no end
I am not your enemy but your friend
No shades of grey can hold me back
I am more complex than white & black

I enrich you whilst enriching myself
My shades of colour are my wealth
I am yellow & orange & golden rays
I am the shine that brightens up your days ❦

'Love'

CHAPTER 8

TO GIVE LOVE IS NOT TO BE LOVED

The gift of love can only be accepted from others once we learn to love self. Learning to love yourself starts with acceptance, recognise your purpose, acknowledge that your flaws along with your talents are what make you who you are. Celebrate being you every day, make no apologies for who you are and embrace your entire being.

GIFT OF LOVE

You enticed me with your gifts so precious they couldn't be
    touched or seen
In the moment I tasted them I wanted to go where you had been
Retrace every footprint of your life's journey
Every morning I'd wake up an hour early
Just to indulge myself in the gift of watching you sleep
When I lay down beside you into your dreams I'd creep
I took each gift you offered readily
Held on to your every movement eagerly
Each time your lips parted to speak my name
It was like a new gift I grabbed feeling no shame
I was like a lap dog lapping you up and breathing you in
Accepting the gifts you gave me was like a wicked sin
But I was out of control under your spell
Never stopping for long enough to dwell
On my obsession with the gifts you offered me
I was so blinded by your beauty I couldn't see
That slowly but surely you were drifting away
Each visit, a little less time you'd stay
The gifts reducing one by one
Until I was left with none
When you failed to return my embrace
I tried to handle the situation with dignity and grace
But I was like an addict gone cold turkey
Angry you weren't there to hear my plea
For one last delicious taste of your gift
A moment of pleasure to uplift
And make me whole just one more time
In my dreams the feeling is divine
I hear them saying that your gifts are cursed
But I say they need to taste them first ❧

UNCONVENTIONAL LOVE

Too little too late to start over again
But as I look at you I remember when
We first connected not sexually
But mentally and spiritually

You were my thesaurus and I your encyclopaedia
I was your audience and you my multi media
You conquered by phobias and I your fears
I eased your sorrow and you shed my tears

You taught me how to love myself
I taught you in self-respect there's a wealth
You stimulated my mind
When you were lost I was your find

You caressed my soul
I became your goal
You understood my position
I overstood your vision

You were my laughter
I was your happily ever after
You were my smile
I was your style

You took me up when I was standing still
I was your determination when you lost your will
You caught me when I thought I was falling
I came to you before I heard you calling

You'd start a sentence and I'd finish it off
I'd give you water before you'd even cough
You blessed me before I even sneeze
I am the door to your keys

We were fine until it became sexual
That's when we stopped acting natural
That's when the rules all changed
And everything we had connected got rearranged

It should have been beautiful
We were supposed to be invincible
But we were sexually incompatible
And everything else became impossible

All that we had done became undone
Our two could no longer be one
Perhaps if we had stayed best friends
This wouldn't be how it ends

But society dictates that we must conform
To a false version of what is norm
We fell into the trap of how it's supposed to be
Instead of simply focusing on you and me

Recognising that what we had was more than enough
And embracing our unconventional love ✤

INSPIRATIONAL LOVE

You are inspirational
Truly sensational
A psychic visionary
A warm hearted missionary
True to yourself
Your creativity and wealth
In itself
Deeper than an ocean
As intriguing as a magic potion

You are intellectually adept
And with your embrace I wept
Even before you embraced me physically
You indulged me intellectually
With no tactile contact at all
You touched me in a way I will always recall

Through your eyes I saw the rain
In the tone of your voice I heard your pain
And when you looked at me
It was as though I could see
Right into your heart
Your life flashed before me from the start

Your spirit touched base with mine
And the sensation was divine
Two kindred souls
Aiming for the same goals

Through your perception
I felt a connection
Out of your vocal composition
I understood your position

And where others might have made eye contact
We made mind contact
And where others may have flirted
We were mentally alerted
To each other's physicality
Feasting on each other's spirituality

Instead of going on a date
We came together like fate
And instead of a restaurant dinner
We got substance from the soul inner
Instead of getting intimate
We got into it
With soul, body and mind
And I never thought I would find
My kindred spirit, burning like a candle in the night
A solitary flame bringing me magic light
Warming me, heating up my soul
Like burning embers on hot coal

And when you touched me there
It was almost too much to bear
In that moment I wanted to drink you in
See what you have seen
Go where you have been

Dine on you like the last supper
Nurse you like a hot cuppa
Soothe you with positive perceptions
Caress you with intricate interceptions
Melt into your body
Like brown sugar in black coffee
Become the object of your desire
Be someone to inspire

And instead of lust
I felt trust
Instead of an urge
I felt a surge
Of pure ecstasy
Knowing that you were in love with me
And I with you ❧

GIFT WRAPPING MY LOVE FOR YOU

Loving you is a pain that cuts deep into my heart
Hurtling through my arteries, tearing it apart
Violently severing it in two
So a part of me is forever with you

Loving you is a torture chamber that entraps my mind
Distorting my inner vision, leaving all thoughts outside of you
    behind
I want to prove that the love I have reserved for you
Can take away your fears, your sorrows, and your blues

I want to gift wrap my love for you
So you can keep it within view
I want to capture nature in its beauty
And wrap it in magic moments so you can see
How it can be, sharing each moment passionately
Embracing love in its entirety

I gather spring blossom from an apple tree
I gather nectar from a honey bee
I gather tropical breezes from the deep blue sea
I gather the first wondrous sounds of a new born baby

I gather the sunset in the twilight sky
I gather the twinkling stars from way on high
I gather a flock of turtle doves flying by
I gather the moonlight reflecting in your eye

I place them gently in a box made of dreams
And scatter a sprinkling of midday sunbeams
I seal it shut with a stream of carob kisses
And wrap it up in a child's birthday wishes

Just to ensure that you know it's from me
I sign my name across it in mango coated candy
Too delicate to handle I send it in a rainbow vision
To meet you serenely in your sleep of indecision

You've taken a portion of my heart and my mind as well
So in my soul I wait at the entrance to hell
In case you don't accept this previous gift of mine
That I tried so hard to make irresistibly divine

For if you don't accept this token of my love
I'm certain that my heart will sadly have had enough
And it will be time for me to retire
From this life that has no place for my passion and desire
But for now I'll just perch on the edge of time
Hoping before eternity our love will be sublime
Content in the knowledge that I gift wrapped my love for you
And packed enough in the box to last your whole life through

Content in the knowledge that I gift wrapped my love for you. ✤

SPIRITUAL CONNECTION

I've got to stop – inhale
It's like a fairy tale
You wouldn't even find it
In a love movie script

We travelled on different planes of the matrix
We passed each other and we didn't even flex
But like some magnetic power in play
We threw reality into disarray

We drew each other together
Like a last endeavour
And then we had to stay
Couldn't just walk away

It was like you were an element of me
And I of you, but we couldn't see
Gliding on a sudden breeze
We came together like a winter freeze
You tell me 'bless you' before I even sneeze

You start a sentence, I finish it off
You pat me on the back before I even cough
You think a thought and I hear it before you speak
It's a spiritual connection
Not a freak situation
Cos you drew me to you with elation
And now we're basking in jubilation
That I found you and you found me
And it's as though I can see
Right into your soul
Like we were supposed
To fulfil a mutual role

We try to walk away
But mentally, we're willing each other to stay

You bind my inner spirit
The ribbon of life connected to it
And the beat of my heart
That should never be apart

We fit together like the pieces of a puzzle
And into the crook of your heart I nuzzle
You're a magnetic force
And like a metal pin, I can't divorce
Myself from your aura
We're in a sweet plethora

You placed your hands in mine
And the sensation was divine
And when our lips touched base
It was like coming up trumps with a triple ace

Delicious, exhilarating
Like a new-born's first tasting
With your physical embrace
I felt my heart race
From my head to my toes
Then I know no where it goes

But in the centre of your mind
I sense I will find
My sweet soul mate
We came together like fate

And now I'm just sitting here
Feeling what happened back there
Breathing it in without a care
Like spring blossom in the air

And it's better than ecstasy
And you haven't even made love to me
Like a multiple spasm
In the ultimate orgasm
A spiritual chasm
An inner soul fathom

Just imagine
That it happened
Like it was meant to be
A peace of you for a peace of me
First piece – mentally
Second piece – spiritually
Third piece - physically

A piece of peace!

Two separate entities
But we were meant to be
Together like birds of a feather
Like rain in stormy weather

I can't think of anything but you
And I don't know what to do
I'm walking in a daze
And the outer world's just a haze
And I want to raise
Myself and drift to you
And I know you feel it to

Cos it's a mind blowing interjection
It's a spiritual connection! ✶

'Ribbon of Life'

CHAPTER 9

FLEEING CLIMATE CHANGE, POVERTY AND WAR

Nobody risks their life in their quest for freedom, braving perils and danger, then survive being stuck in limbo in a living hell unless what they are fleeing is far worse. Rather than demonising those who search for a life beyond survival we should be acting with humanity. Seeking safety and pursuing freedom is not a crime.

STORM

Wind howling, shrill in its refrain
Angrily claiming as its domain
A patch of barren poisoned waste land
This is no winter wonderland

For human beings to inhabit
This rotten, decayed place is not fit
As refuge festers, piled up high
Uneasy on the nose and eye

Shredded tents quake in the storm
And fires have become the norm
Flames ignited to ward of the cold
Join forces with the wind, take hold

Make-shift homes from discarded wares
Don't fulfil dreams, can't cast aside fears
Poverty, persecution and war
Fled but now repeat as they face more

Those who label and victimise
Don't hear in the dark night their cries
As the little protected from nature's wrath
Is now ablaze with all in the fire's path

A cycle of rebuilding reclaimed shelter
Impossible to defend from the winter weather
Each week that passes seems like forever
Fraught with hunger, pain and terror

Been through trauma just to be alive
It's not a crime to try to survive
The aid we bring is not a solution
This shanty town's not a resolution

After the police storm – brutalise
Aided by media who stigmatise
And governments who victimise
And the masses believe their lies

Labelling and appointing blame
Instead of feeling shame for this stain
And their lack of humanity
In responding to human tragedy

Fast to erase from mind and heart
What caused this situation from the start
Selective humanity
Exposing their hypocrisy ❧

CRIMES AGAINST HUMANITY

They describe mass migration as a disaster
Work to ensure no happily ever after
Call humans surviving a 'refugee crisis'
They need to open their minds and understand this:

People have been migrating since the start of time
The desire to stay alive is not a crime
Can't be free without justice and equality
Food, water, shelter, warmth & security

Are basic needs not desires of the greedy
They denigrate and label them poor and needy
Calling them a drain on the economy
Scapegoating as the cause of austerity
Say the country's full up so they can't come in
Judge them by their faith and colour of their skin
Endorse occupations and cause climate change
Then have the audacity to act like it's strange

When people are forced to flee war and poverty
Failing to recognise their own hypocrisy
All around people are literally dying
While governments and media keep on lying

Lacking in compassion and integrity
Investing in borders rather than humanity
MPs vote for bombs but not for ending poverty
Invest in war but not in healthcare or equality

Claim to combat terror but disregard the human cost
No minute's silence or national flag for those lives lost
Until these crimes against humanity cease
Until we have freedom, there will be no peace ❧

FREEDOM TO FLY

My dream
It would seem
Gave me Monday Morning Blues
My mind is filled with hazy hues

Of the journey I took in sleep
Part of me wants to weep
Snippets flash in my mind
But the rest I left behind

In Dreamland
Rub the sand
From tired eye
Ask myself why?

Tormented when I went to bed
Remembering, trying to clear my head
But the memory
Of the high sea

Examining the tidal line
Like at a scene of a crime
As I shower I analyse
The wheres and whys

Haunted by that dream
And the tragic scene
Of people seeking safety
Just wanting to be free

So many lives stolen
By cruel waves taken
Uncontrollably I cried
For all that died

But not just in sorrow
As I feel the anger grow
Thinking of the wickedness at play
Anti-migrant rhetoric used to win election day

I watch as a bird soars high
Allowed its freedom to fly
No go home vans
No anti -migrant bans

No border control blocking its flight
If only we were all free to soar at such a height
No barbed wire fences blocking our route
No myths and lies distorting our truth ✦

MAMA WEEPS

Mama weeps, shedding tears of rain – shine
Rainbow droplets of love – divine
Drinks the elements like fine wine
Waiting patiently, older than time

She tries to shield and guide
But weary and tired
Heavy eyelids close a little
Her breath is soft and gentle

But as she dozes
Chaos poses
Destructive, volatile
While Mama sleeps a while

The place that Mama awakens to
Is broken through and through
Is damaged, pained and dying
Her offspring now are crying

But no rainbow healing tears
Can erase their hurt and fears
While Mama slept her earth erupted
Her slumber abruptly interrupted

When her birth seeds were destroyed
Shocked out of sleep, at first annoyed
She then felt a sharp pain in her womb
Signalling her life buds' doom

Shaken, she couldn't stop the quaking
Her spirit wilted, her heart breaking
Her eruption of anguish was volcanic
Causing those left to react in panic

Her elements released, shattered
Mama choked, her seeds scattered
In their selfishness they'd neglected the mother of their birth
Slowly but surely they were killing Mama Earth ❧

Refugees   Welcome

Zita; Poet~Artist~Activist

'Refugees Welcome'

CHAPTER 10

REMEMBERING THOSE WHO HAVE PASSED

Honouring those who went before us; continuing their legacies.

TWENTY YEARS ON; HOW FAR HAVE WE COME?

Twenty years on
How far have we come?
What has been done?
There's too much still wrong

Stephen Lawrence talented and bright
Aspiring architect killed one night
For nothing more than colour of his skin
Justice sought, fought for by his grieving kin

Challenging institutional racism
Exposing police failings and discrimination
Race Relations Amendment Act was created
A public sector duty against such hatred

Yet still no justice as the killers walk free
Black communities are quite rightly angry
Lawrence family continue to fight on
Inspiring others determined and strong

To challenge racism blighting
Lives and futures igniting
Campaigns to bring about equality
Hopeful that through them eventually

A change would come
Now fast forward on
Twenty years on to the present day
Has racism really gone away?

Now how far have we come?
What more must still be done?
Twenty years on and progress is being reversed
By a Government intent on seeing us cursed

With poverty and deprivation
Injustice and discrimination
Scapegoating of black communities
Encouraged by the Coalition's policies

Making cuts that are ideological
Trying to make it impossible
For progression on equality and race
As they reverse not just slow the pace

Stopping, searching, demonising
Barring, blocking, ostracising
Cutting jobs and communities
Failing on their responsibilities and duties

To eliminate race discrimination
With their deliberate division
Between the rich predominately white
And the poorest who have to fight

Just to stay alive
Just to survive
Disproportionately poor and black
With evil smiles that say 'if you're black get back'

Twenty years for partial justice served
Whilst some still don't get punishment deserved
Twenty years and a family are still grieving
While communities still grasp on to hope of believing

That a different reality is achievable
And that an equal society is possible
Yet even as they dream shedding tears of sorrow
It's unbearable not knowing if this tomorrow
Will come during their or their children's time on earth
Even whilst recognising their own great worth
Feeling the pain of being treated as if they're worthless
In a land ruled by those who couldn't care less

That the disease of racism is reducing their life chances
And instead of progression and advances
They face a life of prejudice and discrimination
In this supposedly great nation.

Twenty years later we all deserve to live at ease
Twenty years later Stephen you deserve to rest in peace ❧

TRIBUTE TO GEORGE PADMORE – AFRICAN LIBERATOR

Written for the Unveiling of a Blue Plaque in memory of George Padmore

Black revolutionary, influential thinker
Proud Pan African, Black Liberator
Striving for independence, powerful orator
Fighting for his people, determined campaigner

Descendent from the Ashanti
Born Malcolm Nurse in T&T
In Trinidad a journalist
In USA an activist

Black student leader changing his name to George Padmore
Fighting for equality whilst studying law
In Russia a Communist
And an Internationalist

Negro Bureau of the Communist International Head
Where ever he went George Padmore led
International Trade Union Committee of Negro Workers he
     created
To address oppression, discrimination and hatred

He moved to London collaborating with greats
Like Eric Williams and CLR James, this trio of mates
Educating and empowering for the betterment of the diaspora
Forming a network of thousands throughout the Caribbean and
     Africa

He organised the fifth Pan African Congress
Determined his people wouldn't settle for less
Seeking independence for each African and Caribbean colony
George believed black people in these lands deserved autonomy

Anti-imperialist
Pro-equality journalist
In newly independent Ghana
He became advisor to Nkrumah

Finally experiencing his vision of independent African States
George Padmore will be remembered as one of the late black greats
He was taken too young but left a legacy
For generations to come to strive for equality

To assert our right to self-organisation
And stand up against the institution
Of racism and discrimination
We must recognise his contribution

Without his vision life would not be the same
So what more fitting tribute than to enshrine his name
So people of all races can recognise his contribution
And the benefits he brought from his organisation

Inspirational
Truly sensational
A deep thinking visionary
Great revolutionary
Powerful orator
George Padmore – African Liberator ✤

BERNIE ON THE BUS
A TRIBUTE TO THE LATE GREAT BERNIE GRANT

Written for the Unveiling of a Blue Plaque in memory of Bernie Grant MP

My first encounter with the great Mr Bernie Grant MP
Was one North London morning travelling bright and early
Sat at the back of a bus focussed on getting to work on time
And making ends meet I was greeted by a presence so sublime

Gliding up the aisle like an African King
Was an elder, stately but friendly, walking
As he greeted each passenger one by one
He lit up the bus like a tropical sun

Smiling like an old friend, warm and welcoming
His traditional outfit, regal look, so enticing
As he approached the back row where I was sat
I was captivated by him just like that

Focusing on my face, he wished me a good morning
I responded coyly but couldn't help smiling
I came to look forward to such morning meetings
Brightening up my otherwise dull commutings

At first encounter, I didn't know who he was
But he was like a kind caring uncle at once
I was intrigued listening to a passenger after
Informing another about this delightful stranger

Little could I have known at the time
That my life path would follow a similar line
As a young activist starting out
I didn't encounter many like Bernie about

There were few role models to inspire
But Bernie Grant was one who full of fire
Determination and strong leadership skills
I could look up to, learn and fulfil

What was mapped out as my destiny
To campaign for workers and community
He was a trade union official, councillor, then MP
Fighting for justice, fairness and equality

Campaigning against apartheid and for reparations
Establishing black structures, fighting race discrimination
Inspirational, honest, loyal, fearless and true
I wish I had the opportunity to thank you

Before you were sadly taken – needed you here
I wept at the sad news and remembered where
I first encountered the warmth and wealth of your humanity
A young girl, troubled, sad, who you made feel like somebody

As a trade union and community activist now
Wish I could sit and debate with you the when, where & how
Run by you a few ideas then discuss them for a while
But I'm strengthened just by the memory of that first smile

Of the same generation of my own father and mother
For me and so many others you're like a father figure
I salute you for all you accomplished and achieved
Paving the way for all of us who also believed

In freedom, equality, justice and democracy
I thank you for your respect and love for your community
And for when I was an insecure young girl feeling like a nobody
For brightening up my days of struggle simply by acknowledging me

Bernie Grant Sir, you are a hero
May your legacy live on and grow
Let us all take inspiration from your stance
And belief that everyone deserves an equal chance ⚘

BOB CROW; LIVING LEGEND

In memory of Bob Crow, General Secretary of the RMT Trade Union, UK

He was a living legend, now he has gone
It's up to us all to keep his legacy strong
He was a man of principle
I thought he was invisible
Inspiring and empowering
A force that was towering
Never wavering, strong
Fast to speak out against wrong
He was a leader but a man of the people
He could never be accused of being a sheeple
He led with his conscience and heart
And that's what set him apart
He walked the walk and fought the fights
For equality, justice and rights
In his resolve unwavering
Never about to cave in
He demanded what was just and fair
Full of compassion and care
He stood up for and beside us all
Firm in the mantra divided we fall
He knew that unity is strength
Took his union from strength to strength
Voice for the voiceless
When others couldn't careless
He stood not just for workers
But also for passengers
For justice and equality
For freedom and humanity
There will only be one Bob Crow
But the truth that all who loved him know
Is that if we had one thousand more Bob Crows
Imagine the collective power to oppose
Austerity cuts and poverty
Oppression and inequality

The battle would be won
But sadly we've lost our only one
So we must keep his memory live and direct
It's the best way in which we can honour and respect
The legacy he gifted us through his life's work
And now that he is departed from this earth
Pledge to carry it on to the end
Bob Crow we salute you, dearest friend ❧

TOO BLACK, TOO FEMALE – MISS MARY SEACOLE

Written whilst I was part of a campaign which succeeded in keeping Mary Seacole on the National Schools Curriculum in the UK

Inspirational
Figure historical
Black & female
Ms Mary Seacole

She was voted number one
The greatest black Briton
Then the government suggested
That she shouldn't be included

In school history teachings
Ignoring public feelings
Fifty personalities write a letter
Telling Government they ought to know better

Than to propose her removal from lessons in school
Really Mr Minister! Discrimination's not cool
Over thirty five thousand signed their name
Generating a rebirth of Ms Mary's fame

The Education Minister said Mary must go!
But Deputy Prime Minister said 'No, No, No!'
So started the LibDem versus Tory
Battle regarding Ms Mary's story

Mary's in the news every day
Mr Minister there's just no getting away
You've got to admit, there's something about Mary
A shame that your view's quite contrary

Sixty politicians sign an Early Day Motion
In recognition of Mary's love and devotion
Tending wounded soldiers in the Crimea
So Mr Minister you should stop to see her

Through the eyes of all those in opposition
To your racist and sexist curriculum vision
History is mystory, our story, all stories
Not restricted to the lives of Tories

Is our heroine Ms Mary Seacole
Really too black and too female
To engage, inspire and educate
Taking her place amongst the good and great?

To write away HerStory
You'd have to rewrite history
Centuries of which you'd have to erase
Including the Transatlantic slave trade

Return all that was taken during British Empire
Millions of workers for sale and free hire
Colonial Rule would have to be reversed
Each history 'liesson' would have to be rehearsed

So Mr Minister let schools teach the truth
To nourish the souls and minds of our youth
Don't disregard her because of her gender and race
Do the right thing and give Mary Seacole her rightful place ❧

DIVIDED BY RACE, UNITED IN WAR - GONE BUT NEVER FORGOTTEN

Written for the planned unveiling of the African and Caribbean War Memorial in Windrush Square, London, UK, in honour of those who served in World War I and II.

DIVIDED by race, UNITED in war
Could not have imagined what was in store
First Class soldier, Second Class citizen
Treated as if foe rather than as kin

Volunteers from Africa and the Caribbean
Their efforts in two world wars forgotten
Proudly fighting for 'King and Empire'
Liberty and peace their wish and desire

Mistreated and humiliated
When they ought to have been celebrated
Dispatched to different corners of the world
Contending with isolation and cold

Putting their lives like others on the line
All blood runs deep red just like yours and mine
Proud to serve for the 'Mother Country'
Shoulder to shoulder, onwards to victory

But where are the awards and honour
For those forgotten because of colour?
We're born equal in the eyes of God
Same battle scars and path to victory trod

Risking lives whilst stripped of dignity
But 'Mother Land' after not so kindly
Those fortunate not to have fallen and survived
Could not have anticipated or conceived

That when they returned to help rebuild the country
They'd be abused and treated so badly
Fast to forget their efforts and bravery
'Liberty and Peace' now a mockery

Without justice there can be no peace
All they wanted was for hatred to cease
So they could contribute to society
Live life equally and freely

It's time to erase this ugly stain
So all of us can know the name
Of each and every one that stood
Honour their memory as we should

For those who answered England's calling
For those who survived and those sadly fallen
For every woman and man
Caribbean and African

Who were divided by race whilst united in war
Recognise what they were fighting for
Let us say their names
Not to mask Britain's shame

But to honour and celebrate
Lest we forget the impact of hate
When left unchallenged to fester
As in the days of yester

The best way to honour their legacy
Is to rise up for peace in their memory

Gone but never forgotten ❧

TRIBUTE TO NELSON MANDELA; NOW YOU ARE FREE

This poem was written for and performed at the vigil for Nelson Mandela held in Trafalgar Square the day after he died and performed at the official UK Memorial Service for Nelson Mandela hosted by the South African High Commission and held at St Martin's in the Field, Trafalgar Square, London.

It's been a long walk to freedom but now you are free
Through your quest for freedom you helped others to see
That forgiveness not retribution could bring about healing
You brought hope and love, truly believing

That peace could become a reality
If we all joined as one in unity
You never wavered, standing proud and tall
A positive inspirational role model to us all

It was a long walk to freedom but now you are free
As we celebrate your life we reflect on how it could be
That one man could leave such a huge legacy
To heal not just South Africa but globally

The world is a better place for your love and your passion
You have truly left an everlasting impression
On all the lives you made better or touched
Because of you we learned to have faith and trust

In the ability to overcome and build a better place
Where we are judged on merit not on race
The long walk to freedom for so many is not done
But with the strength you give to us we will carry on

Enriched by the knowledge you imparted on us all
Motivated by your spirit, we shall not fall
Your passing has left a huge gap and sorrow in our hearts
But the best way we can celebrate your life is to impart

The knowledge and humanity we were blessed to receive
By your presence in our lifetimes, helping us to believe
With truth and understanding your showed us the way
So we honour you now on this momentous day

Pay tribute to the man, the father
The activist, the leader
The revolutionary
Teaching humanity
Preaching equality
Truly extraordinary

Dearest Tata Nelson Mandela we salute you
Rest peacefully; we will see your dream through ✺

DARE TO DREAM; A TRIBUTE TO DR MARTIN LUTHER KING

Written for the fiftieth anniversary of the March on Washington and the BARAC UK Campaign: MLK50, Equality in our Lifetime.

Fifty years since the dream Martin Luther King shared with a
    nation
Of equality for all and an end to discrimination
As we reflect fifty years later the question we must now ask
Is what progress have we really made in the half century that's
    passed?
I have a dream of no poverty or deprivation
An end to prejudice, injustice and discrimination
No abuse or harassment causing devastation
Where challenges to these are not met with confrontation

I have a dream that we'll rise up in unity
Act like one strong and determined community
Live in a world of equal opportunity
Where progress is anticipated eagerly

I have a dream of access to jobs and employment
Where we are assessed on our achievement
Where those with the power to decide don't cast judgment
Based on class or gender or age or skin pigment

I have a dream that every one of us each and every day
Will rise up to those blocking us from progressing on our way
That we'll expose the hypocrites and end the moral decay
Be unrelenting in our pursuit of truth, do not just say

I have a dream that the evil of fascism will be no more
That peace will come and there'll be an end to illegal war
That the pursuit of justice is not blocked by biased law
And in all we strive for, equality is at the core

I have a dream that our children will be judged on merit
Where irrespective of colour or class they're given credit
For their skills, ideas and talent, not broken in spirit
That we create a legacy that they're proud to inherit

I have a dream of free access to education
Where knowledge is not barred due to financial situation
Where we can build a firm and secure foundation
For ourselves, our kin and the next generation

I have a dream of sufficient welfare
Free and accessible healthcare
Of a world that's equal and fair
Where those who hold the power hear

I have a dream where we're free to embrace
Our colour, gender, sexuality and race
Where we're not made to feel out of place
Because of disability, status or face

I have a dream where instead of judging by skin
We live side by side, not like enemies, but kin
Where faith and hope, not hatred and ignorance, win
Where we never stop believing or dreaming

I have a dream that we will always dare
To aspire to and dream of a better world where
The quest for liberty outweighs the fear
Of those who are not brave enough to share
Our dream ✻

Zita, Poet—Artist—Activist